ELFEGO BACA

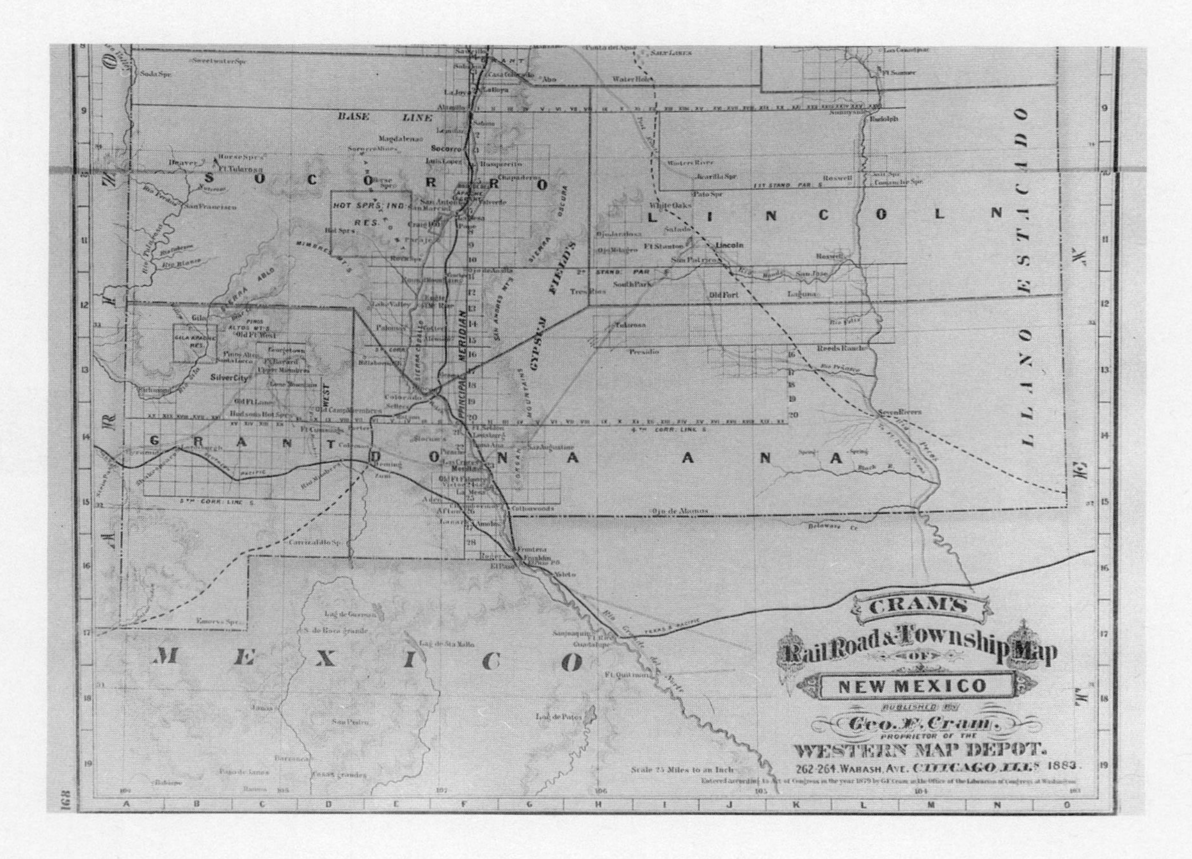
CRAM'S
RailRoad & Township Map
OF
NEW MEXICO
PUBLISHED BY
Geo. F. Cram,
PROPRIETOR OF THE
WESTERN MAP DEPOT.
262-264 WABASH AVE. CHICAGO, ILLS 1883.
Scale 25 Miles to an Inch
SOCORRO
LINCOLN
GRANT
DONA ANA
MEXICO
LLANO ESTACADO
BASE LINE
PRINCIPAL MERIDIAN
GYPSUM FIELDS
HOT SPRS. IND. RES.
Socorro
Lincoln
Silver City
Seven Rivers
Rio Grande del Norte
4TH CORR. LINE S
5TH CORR. LINE S
1ST STAND. PAR. S
2ND STAND. PAR. S
WEST

ELFEGO BACA
IN
LIFE AND LEGEND

by

LARRY D. BALL

THE UNIVERSITY OF TEXAS AT EL PASO

Texas Western Press
The University of Texas at El Paso
El Paso, Texas 79968-0633

First Edition
Library of Congress Catalog Card No. 89-052073
ISBN 0-87404-187-2

All Texas Western Press books are printed on acid-free paper, meeting the guidelines for permanence and durability of the Committee on Production Guidelines for Book Longevity of the Council on Library Resources.

Cover photo: As a district attorney in 1905–1906, Baca attracted the attention of political cartoonists. (From the *Las Vegas Optic,* courtesy Museum of New Mexico

CONTENTS

Preface

This examination of Elfego Baca's life began as an effort to unravel the tangle of events in his encounter with the Texas cowboys at San Francisco Plaza (now Reserve), New Mexico, in 1884. This episode had resulted in the elevation of Baca to heroic status among many of his fellow Hispanos. The remainder of his long life of eighty years appeared rather anticlimactic in the exaggerated light of this single episode. However, even a brief examination of the subsequent events of Elfego Baca's career, as this present work attempts to give, reveals much more substance to it than the 1884 shootout would indicate. That he played a genuine if—somewhat controversial and sometimes less than glorious part—in the history of the modern Southwest is clearly in the record.

The author is indebted to many individuals, libraries, and archives in the preparation of this work. The list is long and includes: John and Cheryl Wilson of Las Cruces, New Mexico; Richard Salazar, New Mexico State Records Center and Archives; the Museum of New Mexico Library; the Socorro Public Library; Special Collections Department, Zimmerman Library, University of New Mexico; Howard Bryan, Albuquerque; Marina Ochoa, Historic-Artistic Patrimony and Archives, Archdiocese of Santa Fe; Bob Dauner, Special Collections Branch, Albuquerque Public Library; Maureen Laue, Assumption Parish, Archdiocese of Kansas; Gary Topping, Utah State Historical Society, Salt Lake City; El Paso Public Library (Texas); the Nita Stewart Haley Library, Midland, Texas; Kansas State Historical Society, Topeka; William E. Unrau, Department of History, Wichita State University, Kansas; and special thanks to Margaret

Daniels and the staff of the Interlibrary Loan Department, Dean B. Ellis Library, Arkansas State University, Jonesboro, for patiently searching out and retrieving many sources necessary for this book. Randall Kesselring, Professor of Economics at Arkansas State University, patiently steered the author through the electronic tangle necessary to prepare the final copy of this manuscript.

I also wish to express my gratitude to my wife, Ruth, who read the manuscript and offered valuable suggestions, and to my son, Larry, Jr., a doctoral candidate at the University of New Mexico, who provided many valuable services on Elfego Baca's home ground.

Larry D. Ball
Arkansas State University

CHAPTER ONE

A SELF-MADE DEPUTY

Elfego Baca's ancestors originated in Spain. They immigrated to the New World by way of Vera Cruz during the Spanish era and settled in present-day Socorro County, New Mexico. Elfego's grandfather, Jose Miguel Francisco Baca, born in 1800, married a member of the Volarde family and established a store in San Marcial, situated about twenty-eight miles south of Socorro. He later relocated the business to Socorro. The 1870 census reported Jose Baca's retail merchandizing business worth $550. Elfego's father, Francisco Baca y Volarde, was born in 1834 and married about 1855. His wife, Juanita, bore him six children: Nestor, the eldest, Abednago, Eloisa, Herminio, Francisco, Jr., and Elfego, the youngest. Although Elfego later asserted that he was born on 27 February 1865, the parish records of the Catholic Church indicate that he was baptized on 15 February 1865 and that he was then five days old, making his birthdate 10 February. Elfego, who enjoyed exaggerating events in his life, declared that his mother gave birth to him while playing *las iglesias*, a game similar to softball, on a field in Socorro.[1]

Francisco Baca's fortunes were uneven in his early years. He amassed considerable property and, according to Elfego Baca, became "one of [the] heavy land-owners and cattle-raisers" in Socorro County. The 1860 census confirms this assertion and lists him as a merchant and farmer, with $600 in personal and $3,500 in real property, a considerable amount of wealth for that day. In 1866 Francisco Baca relocated his family to Topeka, Kansas. His motives for this decision to settle outside the traditional homeland are not clear. Elfego later opined that his father desired to introduce the family to "civilization" and "the benefits of eduction that Socorro did not offer." Abe B. Baca, son of Abednago, Elfego's eldest brother, believed that the Bacas left Socorro to avoid the embarrassment that followed some unspecified financial setback. This reversal of fortunes may have been connected with the dislocations brought about by the Civil War. The destructiveness of the Confederates, ravages of hostile Indians, and scarcity of food prompted many residents to depart Socorro County.[2]

Family members later related to Elfego the story of this adventurous trip to Kansas. The Baca family traveled a road that passed through the future Torrance County and veered northward to link with the Santa Fe Trail. Their ox train moved ponderously, leaving them vulnerable to hostile Indians. These raiders surprised Francisco Baca's night camp near present-day Estancia and kidnapped the baby Elfego. The raiders released him four days later. Elfego did not explain the reason for his liberation. These events took place about the time of his first birthday, in February 1866. The remainder of the journey to Topeka was apparently uneventful. The Bacas may have resided in that part of Topeka which later became Oakland community, the Mexican-American satellite of the Kansas capital.[3]

The Bacas remained in Topeka for fifteen years, according to Elfego's recollections. He said little about his father's activities, except that he worked as a "minor contractor." He may have engaged in horse racing as well, an enterprise that he practiced upon his return to New Mexico. The children profited from Topeka's educational opportunities. Elfego and his elder brother, Abdenago, both used their training in English language to good effect later in New Mexico. Although Elfego belittled the extent of his education—"not much," he quipped many years later—he overstated his ineptitude. Elfego also made a lasting friendship in a schoolmate, Charles Curtis, a young Kaw Indian who later became vice president of the United States in 1929. This extended residence of the Bacas in Topeka was not without family tragedies. In early 1872, Elfego's mother, Juanita, sister, Eloisa, and brother, Herminio, all died within a few weeks of each other, with no documentation surviving that gives the cause. Francisco Baca may have been constrained to break up the family. Abe B. Baca, Elfego's nephew, said that his uncle spent some time in a Topeka orphanage. In the meantime, Francisco Baca and his eldest son, Abednago, sought employment in Colorado.[4]

In 1881, at the age of sixteen, Elfego Baca returned to Socorro to live with an uncle, Estevan Baca. The young man soon found that his many years among the English-speaking residents of Topeka had distanced him from his own people. While he could speak English with scarcely an accent, he could "speak very little Spanish," recalled Baca. "As a matter of fact I was afraid of what they called Mexicans," he admitted. His biographer, Kyle Crichton, says of him:

> Elfego was fifteen and alien in his home town [Socorro]. His Spanish was that picked up from a Spanish household and diffused through the rough hewn English of a Kansas community. It was very poor Spanish, and Elfego was in the position of a man who returns from the war to find his sweetheart afraid of him.

In spite of this handicap, he maintained a strong allegiance to the Spanish-American community throughout his long life.[5]

While working as a vaquero on his uncle's ranch at La Parida, a few miles northeast of Socorro, Elfego Baca claimed to have had a unique experience. He said he became friends with Billy the Kid, the infamous mankiller and participant in the bloody Lincoln County War, in neighboring Lincoln County. Henry McCarty, alias William "Billy the Kid" Bonney, had reportedly killed some twenty-one men. In search of excitement, these adventurous youths visited Albuquerque. No sooner had they arrived, Baca recalled, than they witnessed a senseless killing. A city officer shot an innocent pedestrian in the course of breaking up a disturbance:

> Billy and I were wandering [*sic*] what we were going to do [for excitement] when here comes a policeman and shot a man about five or six times. The policeman went

> into the saloon and called the boys [patrons] to have a drink. About that time here comes [Sheriff] Perfecto Armijo and said, "Who killed that man out there?" The policeman said, "I did, what about it?" Perfecto then . . . picked him [the lawman] up just like a cat will pick up a mouse.[6]

The angry sheriff carried the lawless subordinate off to jail. Baca recalls that the malevolent city officer was later hanged for this vicious crime. This unfortunate murder, which Baca recalled correctly in broad outline, took place on 18 June 1881, when Deputy Sheriff Milton Yarberry shot and killed Charles D. Campbell, a railroad employee. In an ironic turn of events, Sheriff Armijo was later obliged to preside at the hanging of his errant underling.[7]

The two young men then proceeded to Old Town Albuquerque where the prankish Kid proceeded to create a disturbance. According to Elfego Baca:

> Billy carried a little pistol called [a] Bulldog repeater . . . . it made a strong noise perhaps louder than a .45 [calibre] gun. . . .Billy thought the town was more silent than what he expected it [to be]. He then fired a shot up in the air and it made an awful strong noise. Here comes the Deputy Sheriff, a very brave man by the name of Cornelio Murphy. He searched both of us and he was very mad. . . . but he couldn't find a pistol. The Deputy walked away . . . when Billy fired two more shots. . . .The deputy came back as mad as a man could be and searched us again. He called us every name that he could think of.

After a few more pistol shots into the ceiling of the Martinez saloon, this mischievous pair wisely left town. Elfego Baca recalled that his devilsh comrade deceived Deputy Sheriff Murphy by hiding his small handgun in his "stiff, Derby hat." This story may have some foundation in truth since Cornelio Murphy was a deputy of Sheriff Perfecto Armijo at this time.[8]

While Baca no doubt believed that his sometime companion

was *the* Billy the Kid, there is little evidence for this assumption. The infamous mankiller was preoccupied with lawless escapades elsewhere at the time. However, the teenage Hispano may have briefly consorted with another young troublemaker with the sobriquet of "Kid." Several such desperadoes practiced their criminal trades in and around Albuquerque in the early 1880s. Charles Daily, alias Kid, committed horse theft in the vicinity and fled to Santa Fe. On 17 May 1880, officers arrested Daily and returned him to Albuquerque for trial. The "Texas Kid" also spent time in the Bernalillo County Jail, but escaped in this same month. Chester Cousins, alias the Slim Kid, murdered a man in nearby San Marcial two years later. If Elfego Baca did hurrah Albuquerque with someone calling himself Billy the Kid, and there is no reason to doubt his story, this anonymous person could have been one of these three men. Whatever the case, Baca was a witness to much violence in his formative years.[9]

The boys parted company soon after their Albuquerque fling, and Elfego went to work for Francisco Apodaca in Barelas, a few miles southwest of Albuquerque. Elfego and Pedro Apodaca, son of Francisco, transported meat to the Santa Fe Railroad workers. The 1880 census lists Francisco Apodaca, aged fifty-five years, and his son, Pedro, twenty-one at this time.[10]

In 1880 Elfego's father returned to New Mexico to take up the combined pursuits of gambler and peace officer. As town marshal of Belen, in neighboring Valencia County, he soon ran into difficulty. The Santa Fe *Daily New Mexican* reported Policeman Baca in a serious disturbance on Monday, 27 December 1880:

> a party of drunken Mexicans got into a row . . . in the store of F[rederick] Scholle & Co. Pistols were drawn and a policeman, Francisco Baca y Volarde started in to stop the row. The drunken men pitched into the officer and he fired into the crowd, killing Eutimio Baca and wounding Termino Baca, a brother of Eutimio.

The latter victim also soon died.[11]

On 2 February 1881, the *New Mexican* reported that Francisco Baca had been arrested and jailed in Los Lunas, the county seat, to await trial for murder at district court in May. In spite of the efforts of Thomas F. Conway, a highly respected lawyer, the Valencia County jury convicted Francisco Baca of murder in the fifth degree in one of the deaths and sentenced him to a prison term. Since there was no territorial penitentiary the former town marshal was to be transported to the Kansas state prison. The trip was postponed while he awaited trial on the second murder indictment at the fall 1881 term of district court.[12]

Elfego Baca, who concluded that a "powerful family" in Valencia County—perhaps the Lunas—had railroaded his father, began to plan a jailbreak. In late June 1881, Elfego and a young friend named Chavez traveled to Los Lunas on foot with "a total of forty-five cents" between them. The young men approached the jail, which stood a good distance apart from any other structures, probably on the night of 24/25 June. They climbed to the second floor by ladder and, Elfego recalled,

> crept through the easily opened window, and proceeded . . . to saw out a space in the floor large enough for the body of Father Baca to wiggle through from beneath. It was leisurely work. The jailer was gone for the night . . . and they were too far from the habitations of Los Lunas to occasion suspicion by the sawing. . . .
>
> Two fellow prisoners boosted Father Baca through the opening and were in turn boosted and yanked through to freedom.

The newsaper account of the breakout mentions four escapees, rather than the three in Elfego's recollections. The escaping party helped themselves to venison and other condiments from the jailer's clothesline and crossed the road to take refuge in a grassy field. Amply provided with food, they idled the day away watching the embarrassed sheriff, Henry Connelly, and his posse "beat the surrounding country with energy and abandon," recalled Elfego Baca.[13]

While Elfego's account of the jailbreak conforms generally to the facts, he fails to reflect upon the seriousness of the event. Several dangerous criminals were on the loose in New Mexico as a result of a series of recent jail breaks. The Los Lunas breakout compounded this problem, since at least one murderer, John Pearce, was among the four men whom Elfego Baca released. (A second murderer, one Thacker, either refused to escape or Francisco Baca would not permit him to accompany the fleeing party.) The inmates, who had been plotting an escape for some time, had obtained the key to their shackles in advance. The jailer, assuming that he had lost it, had failed to report the disappearance to Sheriff Connelly. The jail "is built of stone," said a *New Mexican* reporter, but "the ceiling consisted merely of [one] inch boards." For persons on the outside, that is, Elfego Baca and his friend, Chavez, it "was no difficult task," continued this newspaperman, to saw a hole through the ceiling. Elfego cleverly scheduled this jail delivery while Sheriff Henry Connelly and his staff were distracted by the festivities surrounding the celebration of the day of San Juan (24 June).[14]

While John Pearce and the other escapees fled northward, the Bacas sought the protection of Francisco's brother in Socorro, Texas, just below El Paso and within easy reach of the safety of Mexico. According to Elfego, Francisco Baca was permitted to return to Socorro, New Mexico, seven years later, in 1888. Presumably, the charges against his father had been dropped. Whether Sheriff Connelly ever suspected the involvement of Elfego in the jail delivery is not known. After the rescue of Francisco Baca, Elfego obtained a clerking job in the Socorro store of Juan Jose Baca, whom the new employee characterized as a "big merchant." Elfego may have begun to read law in his spare time.[15]

In November 1882, the voters of Socorro County went to the polls in general elections. As sheriff they elected Pedro Simpson, a well-educated young man whose mixture of Anglo and Hispanic backgrounds appealed to a wide range of voters. Simpson had taken on a difficult task, since Socorro County was undergoing rapid economic development. The new Santa Fe Railroad had introduced large numbers of rough, itinerant workers into the region, while mining property and cattle ranges were being developed in the western precincts. Many of the new arrivals were Texans who held the native community in very low esteem.

These herders enjoyed riding recklessly through Socorro and other communities and shooting their weapons indiscriminately at any moving object.[16]

One such incident, in January 1883, may have brought about Elfego Baca's introduction to the legal side of law enforcement. Several young cowboys attempted to "tree" the county seat. Sheriff Simpson pursued them out of town and in the direction of Escondido, three miles north of the county seat. Many years later, Elfego informed a Works Projects Administration interviewer that he joined this chase:

> I had gone to Escondida . . . to visit my uncle. A couple of Texas cowboys had been shooting up the town of Socorro. They hadn't hurt anybody that time. Only frightened some girls. That's the way they did in those days—ride through town shooting at dogs and cats. . . .The Sheriff came to Escondida after them. By that time they were making a couple of Mexicans dance [in Escondido], shooting up the ground around their feet. The Sheriff said to me, "Baca, if you want to help, come along, but there's going to be shooting."

"We rode after them," added Baca, "and I shot one of them [from] about three hundred yards away."[17]

On 25 January a Socorro correspondent of the *Daily New Mexican* reported this tragic event, but failed to name the posseman who fired the fatal shot. The victim, a cowhand in his early twenties named Townsend, hailed from Brownwood, Texas. A second member of this band had been wounded but got away. Townsend lingered a short time before dying. Although he complained bitterly about the failure of his friends to return for him, the dying man refused to divulge their names. Frank Collinson, another Texas cattleman who happened to be in Socorro during this fracas, regarded the shooting as senseless. "There was no harm in any of them," he averred. He declared that Sheriff Simpson and an unnamed deputy permitted the horsemen to ride out of town and only then took up pursuit. "They did not attempt to arrest the boys," wrote the cattleman, "but commenced to shoot at them" from behind. "It was a wanton killing," charged

Collinson. When someone later asked Elfego the name of the dead man, he admitted that he did not know. The horseman "wasn't able to tell me by the time I caught up with him," said the posseman in a bit of hardened jest.[18]

If this service in the sheriff's posse was Elfego Baca's first law enforcement act, he soon acquired other opportunities. While clerking in the Jose Baca store, Elfego met Pedro Sarracino, brother-in-law and business partner of Jose Baca. Sarracino informed Elfego about clashes between the Hispanos of San Francisco Plaza, a settlement some 130 miles to the west, and newly arrived Anglo cattle interests. Sarracino managed a store there and also served as a deputy of Socorro County Sheriff Pedro A. Simpson. Sarracino complained that the cowboys not only bullied inoffensive townspeople but went so far as to castrate one Hispano, nicknamed El Burro, and used another, Epitacio Martinez, for target practice, wounding him four times. The young clerk expressed anger and dismay as such brutalization. When the deputy sheriff added that the stockmen threatened his life if he attempted an arrest, Elfego scolded the hesitant deputy:

> I told Sarracino . . . that he should be ashamed of himself, having the law on his side, to permit the cowboys to do what they did [castrate a man]. He told me that if I wanted to, I could take his job. I told him that if he would take me back to Frisco [Plaza] with him I would make myself a self-made deputy.[19]

Since this conversation in October 1884, much mystery has surrounded his official status and the purpose for the long trip to Frisco Plaza. Many people believe that he was campaigning for his superior, Sheriff Pedro Simpson, who was seeking re-election in the following month. Baca denied this in a WPA interview in the 1930s. "Hell, I wasn't electioneering," he said gruffly, "I don't know where they got that idea. . . .I couldn't have made a speech to save my life." Abe B. Baca, nephew of Elfego, averred that the young man accompanied Deputy Sarracino in order to visit a girlfriend, a member of the Armijo family. Elfego apparently concocted the story of this "self-designated" deputyship late in life. It appears for the first time in writing in the *Political*

Record of 1924. A 1912 sketch says that "Sheriff Simpson appointed Mr. Baca [as] a deputy" and that he (Baca) traveled to San Francisco Plaza in that capacity.[20]

There is no doubt that Sheriff Simpson issued Elfego Baca a deputy's badge, although the circumstances of the commission are unclear. A handwritten commission exists in the papers of Napoleon B. Laughlin, a distinguished New Mexico lawyer and Elfego Baca's defense attorney at his trial for the murder of a cowboy in San Francisco Plaza. This document was later presented as "defense exhibit A." Part of the heading has disappeared, but the body reads:

> [I, P. A. Simpson, Sheriff] of Socorro County by these presents [*sic*] appointed Elfego Baca deputy sheriff for and in Socorro county and hereby authorise him to act in such capacity from and after this 26th day of Oct. 1884.
>
> [Signed] P. A. Simpson
> Sh. Soc. Co.

With badge in hand, Baca boarded Pedro Sarracino's mule-drawn buckboard for the 130-mile trip to San Francisco Plaza. This novice lawman apparently arrived late on 27 October or early the following day. The journey was difficult at best, and the two passengers had to assist the overburdened animal to "climb every steep hill," recalled Baca.[21]

By this time, western New Mexico had begun to attract many investors in cattle and mining enterprises. In Socorro County's westernmost precincts the mining camps of Mogollon and Cooney, among others, were producing appreciable quantities of mineral wealth. In the grasslands of the valley of the San Francisco River, which trailed off southwestward to the Gila River, large cattle herds had begun to form in the early 1880s. Among these new spreads was the Spur, owned by brothers named Hall. William Slaughter's WIL S Ranch was situated near present-day Quemado. His brother, John Benjamin Slaughter, was located to the south, near the headwaters of the San Francisco. (This latter Slaughter is not to be confused with John Horton Slaughter, founder of the San Bernardino ranch in southern

Arizona.) Two Englishmen, Harold C. Wilson and Montague Stevens, possessed a spread two miles north of Alma, hence the name WS. James H. Cook, an adventuresome young man in his twenties, served as general manager. Stevens also ranged a large herd far to the northeast near Horse Springs, in the American Valley. John W. Cox, another Englishman and former sergeant in the Eighth United States Cavalry, ran a herd on the Tularosa, a small tributary of the San Francisco River.[22]

In the midst of these many enterprises was San Francisco Plaza, on the upper San Francisco River. With a population of 271 persons in the 1880 census, this settlement actually consisted of three hamlets—Upper, Middle, and Lower Plaza—only short distances apart. Postmaster James Logan served all three. While these villages were heavily Hispanic in 1884, discharged United States soldiers had reportedly established the first settlement at Upper Plaza early in the previous decade. Some ex-bluecoats intermarried with the local native families, whose livelihoods consisted of farming and sheepherding. Among the former soldiers was Dan Milligan, owner of a combination store and saloon in Upper Plaza. Milligan was a striking figure of over six feet. "His hands were the largest I have ever seen," wrote William French, who noted "a fringe of hair some six or eight inches long on an otherwise bald head." Law enforcement consisted of Justice of the Peace Lopez and Deputy Sheriff Pedro Sarracino, who represented Peter A. Simpson in the distant county seat of Socorro.[23]

Dan Milligan's emporium in Upper Plaza attracted many cowboys who enjoyed his whiskey on Saturday night. Drunken herders became a common sight. These rowdies enjoyed "treeing" the town, by riding through Upper Plaza's single street and firing their pistols at conspicuous targets, to include houses, chickens, hogs, and other prominent features. Gunfights were not uncommon. Charles "Dutch Charlie" Schneider took the life of one Gereen in an argument over a debt. Rancher John Cox was wounded by one of Schneider's stray bullets. In May 1884, newspapers reported that a ranch employee shot and killed a man (a German) in Frisco Plaza. In the fall reports reached Socorro, and Elfego Baca, about the castration of El Burro and the wounding of Epitacio Martinez. While such violence appeared senseless a more serious purpose may have lurked beneath the surface. Some confrontations were provoked by the intrusion of cattle and other livestock upon farm and garden plots. Although a territorial fence law existed, some confusion existed over its provisions and the statute had not been well enforced.[24]

This cattleman's "invasion" of Socorro County also threatened the traditional county political machine. The few Anglos who had resided for some time in this heavily Hispanic county had long since reached an accommodation with the older residents. Some, such as Sheriff Simpson, publicized his reconciliation by hispanicizing his name to Don Pedro. The newly arrived stockmen desired to oust Don Pedro and other officeholders, and the cattlemen designated the November 1884 elections as the appropriate time. William French, the English visitor at the WS Ranch, recalled that this determination increased all the more when Sheriff Simpson failed to protect a prisoner from vigilantes in the county seat. In January 1884, Joel Fowler, a cattleman (and Texan), was the victim. While few doubted that Fowler was a psychotic killer, he was nonetheless from the Lone Star State. Not only had the sheriff failed to protect this prisoner, but the lawman had killed another Texas cowhand under questionable circumstances the preceding January. Political enemies also charged that Simpson was guilty of malfeasance in office.[25]

Elfego Baca in 1883, the year before his confrontation with the cowboys in San Francisco Plaza. (Photo by Edwin A. Bass, courtesy Museum of New Mexico)

CHAPTER TWO

THE BACA-COWBOY WAR

Whatever Elfego Baca's reason for the visit to San Francisco Plaza in October, his confrontation with the Texas cowboys in this remote community became a memorable event in New Mexico history. This rencontre, in which two men died, has been called by various names: "The Mexican War," "Shootout at Frisco Plaza," "The Baca-Cowboy War," or simply, "Baca's Battle." The events that took place in those five days, from 28 October to 1 November 1884, have been overshadowed by the spectacular concluding shootout between Elfego Baca and the cattle interests. The authority of the law had been in serious doubt for some time in that area, and the prospects of a collision between the growing Anglo stock-raising enterprises and the settled Hispanic sheep and farming community were very great.

Since those eventful days, the accounts of several eyewitnesses and participants have provided the standard record of "the Mexican War." In addition to Elfego Baca's *Political Record* and the biographical effort of Kyle Crichton, the recollections of James H. Cook and William French have served as the primary sources for the Frisco incident. Cook, the foreman of the WS Ranch at Alma, was a spokesman for the stockmen during the confrontation. Although he naturally reflects the cattlemen's point of view, Cook wrote many years after the confrontation and occasionally expressed some admiration for Baca. William French, the Englishman, was also present. He and other fellow

Englishmen were guests of the WS. He later succeeded James H. Cook as foreman of the WS. French wrote with tongue in cheek, but his pages provide some valuable details. Perhaps some participants deserved caricature since the alcohol flowed freely during those tense days. The details of the Englishman's account could hardly have been invented. James Cook mentions the presence of "English friends" in Frisco Plaza, but fails to provide their names. Cook probably referred to Montague Stevens and Alfred Hardcastle, both Englishmen, who were present in Frisco Plaza. Unfortunately, their accounts of the shootout are very brief.

Newspaper coverage of the Frisco shooting was very sketchy, since western Socorro County was far off the main roads. V. B. Beckett, editor of the Chloride *Black Range*, reported (if inaccurately) the initial bloodshed. Through a stroke of good fortune, the *Albuquerque Evening Democrat* attempted full coverage of Elfego Baca's trial, on 8-9 May 1885, for the deaths of two cowboys at Frisco Plaza. This anonymous reporter made a verbatim report of part of the proceedings. Baca's testimony represents his earliest rendition of the Frisco incident and provides a good corrective to the later embellished versions. Testimony of other participants also gives useful details. Unfortunately, the reporter was unable to attend one day of the trial, thus a portion of it was not recorded. Some valuable data about these proceedings are preserved in the Napoleon B. Laughlin Papers. Laughlin, a prominent lawyer and legislator, was one of Baca's defense attorneys and later an associate justice of the New Mexico Supreme Court.[26]

No sooner had young Deputy Baca arrived in San Francisco Plaza than his services were required on the morning of 28 October. Baca later testified at his trial that Charles McCarthy, a herder for the Slaughter ranch, fired his revolver in Dan Milligan's saloon in Upper Plaza. I "started out immediately to do my duty," continued Baca, and "arrested him." In the absence of a justice of peace in this village, the deputy escorted him to Middle Plaza for trial. It appears that McCarthy paid his fine and was released, but he was soon in trouble again. Baca testified:

> at 2 o'clock I was at Milligan's, and McCarthy, my [former] prisoner, commenced firing off his revolver, at every-

Socorro, New Mexico, about the time that Elfego Baca set off for San Francisco Plaza in 1884. (Photo by J.R. Riddle, courtesy Museum of New Mexico)

As a clerk in Juan José Baca's store, Elfego Baca learned about the atrocities committed by cowboys in San Francisco Plaza. The store is shown abandoned, about 1920. (Courtesy Museum of New Mexico)

> thing and everybody; Milligan went out [of his store] yelling; he knew I was a deputy sheriff, and asked me to help hm; when I asked McCarthy to stop . . . he fired the last of the five shots at me; then I went home and got some men to help me arrest him, because I had no arms at the time; I got eight or nine men and went back to Milligan's house and did not find McCarthy there.

The posse eventually arrested McCarthy on a nearby ranch road.[27]

What began as the antics of a drunken cowhand soon took on threatening implications. Baca obtained Montague Stevens's carriage to carry the prisoner to Middle Plaza, where the deputy placed McCarthy under guard in a private residence. The cowboy "abused us in a very insulting manner," recalled Baca. In addition, "a large number of cowboys" gathered, some of whom accompanied the official party to Middle Plaza. They were miffed at this insulting treatment of one of their own. Montague Stevens recalled that getting drunk, yelling, and firing weapons in the streets was the "custom of the country." There was "Nothing [the] matter with that." While in Middle Plaza, McCarthy again attempted to kill the deputy sheriff with the gun of the Slaughter ranch foreman, Young Parham. Baca later admitted in court that his attitude hardened toward Charles McCarthy after this second attempt on his life:

> he [McCarthy] drew Perham's [Young Parham] pistol and shot it at me; I then refused to let him off or have any bail; Sorcino [Pedro Sarracino?] and [Young] Parham were willing to be his bondsmen, and at first I concluded to let him out on bail; had three or four lines of [the] bond written when [Dan] Milligan came in, very drunk and insulting; he rapped on the counter and said that no bond should be allowed in McCarthy's case; I then had the prisoner placed in a house in town and guarded.[28]

At this point Dan Milligan, the complainant, suddenly had a change of heart. He inexplicably demanded that Baca release the cowboy. While his motives are unclear, it appears he feared a loss of business, or possibly the presence of the John B. Slaughter hands intimidated him. Alcohol may have simply fogged his mind. The peace officer remained firm. The barkeeper returned at midafternoon and again three hours later with the threat that he "had arms to rescue the prisoner," meaning "a large number of cowboys." Baca replied that such bullying "did not make any difference" and added firmly that Milligan "would not take McCarthy away from me in any manner." When the inebriated saloon man refused to go away,

> I [Baca] then drew a pistol and fired a shot into the ground to see if he would go; he said; 'You are a bad shot; you didn't hit me;' I told him that I didn't want to shoot anybody, and that I wanted him to go away; he said that he would go away, and started to go where his horses were hitched; [but] he returned soon and talked very insultingly; I again told him to go away; that he was making me 'tired'; then he mounted his horse and again dismounted, came back and said: "The devil may take me if I don't get Charley McCarthy out."[29]

By this time, tempers had become explosive. Deputy Sheriff Baca was unwilling to tolerate more bullying. When Milligan made this last remark, he and the herders in his party apparently made some threatening moves toward their weapons. Baca's trial testimony about this episode is unfortunately cryptic. He merely remarks that "I then ordered the guards to fire, and the two discharges went off about the same time—their fire and our fire." In his *Political Record*, published in 1924, Baca elaborated on this encounter in Middle Plaza, but with obvious exaggerations not related at his trial:

> That night [28 October] twelve cowboys demanded the release of the man I had under arrest. They were armed to the teeth. I told them that instead of releasing the prisoner I was going to give them time enough to count from one to three before I shot. They undertook to draw their weapons; then I started "one, two, three" and

> fired. When I fired they ran. I killed one man and horse on the run. I hung on to my supposed prisoner.[30]

The first newspaper to report this shooting, the Chloride *Black Range*, reflected the cattleman's point of view. Young Parham, foreman of the Slaughter ranch and Charles McCarthy's immediate superior, said this journalist,

> went to Baca and asked that his man be tried, fined and set at liberty at once, as he [Parham] needed his services, but his request was refused, and it is claimed that with few more words fire was opened on Perryman [Parham] from a dozen or more guns which constituted Baca's guard. Perryman, who was on horse-back, wheeled and fled when the shooting began, and although the range was short the shots not less than fifty, not a bullet struck him. His horse, however, was killed under him, and the animal . . . struck the ground with his rider underneath, crushing Perryman so badly that at last accounts his life was despaired of.

The stockmen enjoyed any opportunity to criticize the marksmanship of the Hispanos. James Cook, an Alma rancher who arrived two days later, recalled that another member of the cowboy mob, Tabe Allen, was shot in the knee. Parham died from complications arising from his injuries.[31]

Several facts emerged from this first day of action in San Francisco Plaza. Charles McCarthy, the Slaughter cowhand, was very drunk, very elusive, and very dangerous. He attempted to shoot the deputy sheriff on two occasions. Dan Milligan's inconsistent role—the complainant and then the defender of McCarthy—is puzzling, although he, too, was evidently inebriated. (It is tempting to conclude that the reporter who copied Elfego Baca's testimony erroneously wrote Milligan but meant Parham.) The deputy sheriff did not stand alone against the mob on this day, the twenty-eighth. A *posse comitatus* assisted him. Baca wrote in the 1920s that only one man, Francisquito Naranjo, agreed to aid him in the arrest of McCarthy. Baca also implied that he stood alone in the shootout with Parham's group.[32]

The twenty-ninth of October was largely uneventful. The cattlemen employed this day to muster their forces, while Deputy Baca stubbornly held on to his prisoner in Middle Plaza (in spite of one more brief escape). The afflicted cattlemen sent out a call for assistance against a possible Hispano uprising. James Cook, the WS foreman, recalled that a cowboy rode up to his home "at a furious gait" in the evening and reported that "the Mexicans had gone on the warpath." They intended, said the messenger, "to wipe out all the Americans" in the vicinity. He asked for assistance to protect the ranchers in and around San Francisco Plaza. William French also received this summons, possibly from the same rider. A trail-weary horseman arrived at the WS ranch in the afternoon, presumably on 29 October. He informed the Englishman and others that a cowboy had been killed and that "the Mexicans were holding another [McCarthy] in captivity. . . . It was feared an attack would be made on some of the outlying ranches." This messenger was destined for Alma, the location of the nearest Anglo deputy sheriff, Dan Bechtol. The cattlemen desired Bechtol's presence to lend official color to their acts and to counter the Hispano lawman, Elfego Baca. The WS contingent, including French and other Englishmen, reached the SU ranch, near the Plaza, about one o'clock on the morning of 30 October. Deputy Bechtol's party arrived shortly thereafter. In the words of French, the latter group was "full of zeal and whiskey." The entire aggregation discussed plans for several hours and "got no further rest that night." The absence of rest and the presence of abundant alcoholic beverages reflected upon the conduct of the stockmen the next day.[33]

The size of the cattlemen's party remains unclear. Justice of the Peace Lopez informed Elfego Baca that some 150 herders resided in the area, although this full contingent never assembled in Frisco Plaza. James Cook says "quite a crowd" had assembled by daylight. William French believed that "twenty or thirty" rode into the plaza on that day. Jerome Wadsworth, one of the cowboy minutemen, testified at Baca's trial that "forty-five or fifty" comprised their party. Baca later wrote that about eighty cowboys gathered, although this is probably an exaggeration. His obituary—Baca died 27 August 1945—continued to publicize this exaggerated figure. Montague Stevens opined that there were not that many herders in the region. No doubt the number of participants varied from day to day and some distinction should be made between lookers-on and active troublemakers. The estimates of French and Wadsworth were probably closer to the truth.[34]

The cattlemen "presented quite a formidable appearance as we rode into the plaza" on the thirtieth, wrote William French, having "slept in their clothes for several nights and none having shaved." As these fierce-looking horsemen drew up at Milligan's emporium, says French, "we found the place almost deserted." The stockmen soon learned that "the entire population had migrated to the middle plaza." This discreet withdrawal may have been the result of Deputy Sheriff Elfego Baca's order that women and children take refuge in the church of Middle Plaza. James Cook admitted the inhabitants of the three hamlets were alarmed and feared that the cowboys intended "to clean out the Mexicans." He learned that "all the Mexicans living within a day's ride" had been summoned. While it is unclear how many responded to this clarion call, some anxious persons did congregate on hillsides around the Plaza later in the day.[35]

The stockmen were slow to muster their forces on the morning of 30 October. Deputy Sheriff Dan Bechtol arose tardily at mid- morning, still feeling the effects of the previous night's binge. The presence of his badge was important as official cover for any cowboy endeavor on behalf of Charles McCarthy. William French also refers to a twenty-mile ride after rising, in order to obtain the services of an Anglo justice of the peace. This precinct official was apparently William W. Wilson, who resided in Tularosa (present-day Aragon), and who later participated in judicial proceedings against Elfego Baca. The cowhands desired to ensure McCarthy "a fair trial" before an Anglo justice of the peace rather than "being carried off to Socorro." The cattlemen designated James Cook as one of their leaders. He accepted reluctantly. They held a "council of war" at which it was decided to dispatch a "committee of two" to inquire about McCarthy's location and legal status. An erroneous report circulated that the Hispanos had by now murdered McCarthy.[36]

This committee, consisting of Jerome Wadsworth and Clement Hightower, conferred with Baca about eight o'clock that morning, 30 October. Jerome Wadsworth testified in Baca's trial that as his committee rode into Middle Plaza,

> Mr. Baca challenged him and asked if he was friend or foe; that he assured [Baca] he was a friend; that they [the cattlemen] had heard that Chas. McCarthy was dead and they wanted to see him; that Mr. Baca said that if they would sign an agreement that he, Baca, would not be harmed that day he would [produce?] McCarthy and he might have a trial.

Baca, who erroneously refers to Wadsworth as Gyrone Martin in his memoirs, declared many years later that the two stockmen cautiously negotiated at a distance of two hundred yards. "I commenced to play with my two guns in their direction," boasted Baca. They merely proposed that Baca should take his charge to Upper Plaza for trial that day. The lawman consented and the two sides composed a written agreement, in Spanish, to that effect and bound the cattlemen to avoid harming the deputy and his posse. A brief delay occurred when the posse refused to accompany Elfego Baca into the cowboy stronghold. When the cowboy delegation "promised that they would not hurt the guards or me," recalled Baca, the possemen agreed to escort Charles McCarthy. Some anxious moments occurred when the official party met two surly cowboys on the road to Upper Plaza. Both parties took opposite sides of the road and avoided a clash. About an hour elapsed during these negotiations and the trip to Upper Plaza.[37]

The circumstances surrounding the trial of the disturber of the peace, Charles McCarthy, are very confused. The precise truth of this critical event is probably lost. Deputy Baca cordially greeted the cattlemen's party at the home of Justice of the Peace Lopez, "Good Morning, gentlemen." William French, who witnessed this event, observed Baca in conference with Deputy Sheriff Bechtol and the Anglo justice of the peace and his Hispano counterpart. In his trial testimony, Elfego Baca declared he had begun a list of witnesses to be summoned and placed it in the hands a temporary deputy, J. Parozia. Suddenly, Parozia "saw a lot of men [cowboys] coming" toward the courtroom and expressed the fear that they intended Baca and the posse harm. Baca agreed, noting that the herders had "arms in their hands." James Wadsworth observed this approach of his fellow cattlemen. At Baca's trial, Wadsworth recalled that the deputy intended to place Charles McCarthy in custody of the cattlemen's committee, apparently until the justice of the peace was ready for the trial. "McCarthy was standing just outside the door, and remarked," said Wadsworth, "look at the crowd of men [cattlemen] coming here." Wadsworth added voluntarily that "they were all armed."[38]

James Cook led this party, which included several drunken and boisterous individuals. Among these loudmouths was one named Wilson. The identity of this person is unclear, since several Wilsons were present including the justice of the peace and an Englishman, Harold C. Wilson, owner of the WS ranch. It appears that Baca or Posseman Geronimo Armijo had arrested yet another Wilson with another man for disturbing the peace. Baca instructed Armijo to release them. Baca wrote later that he was acquainted with this troublemaking Wilson and addressed him cordially, "Hello, Mr. Wilson," "Hello, you little Mexican, etc., etc.," replied the stockman. Baca noted at his trial that Wilson insulted him and "said he didn't want to talk to me. . . . I then drew my pistol and told him that I did not want to talk to him either." The deputy sheriff wrote later that during this exchange of insults, one of the Cook party fired a weapon at him. "I don't think he intended to shoot me," admitted Baca, "because there were some more [innocent] people in back of me." James Cook, who regretted Wilson's abusive remarks about Baca, recalled this gunfire. "One of the young men in our party in some manner fired his gun accidentally," said Cook. William French, who witnessed this moment, says nothing about a threatening crowd. He added that the trial took place, that the judge fined Charles McCarthy five dollars, and he emerged a free man "surrounded by his friends." The proceedings took about thirty minutes, after which French and his English compatriots were then "formally introduced" to the man who was the focal point of so much attention.[39]

In the meantime Deputy Sheriff Baca had disappeared after the confrontation with the Cook mob. The unknown herder's shot apparently convinced him that the cowboys truly intended mischief. James Wadsworth observed Baca's abrupt departure and testified that when the deputy saw the approaching cattlemen, "Mr. Baca stepped out the back door" of the justice's office. "That was the last seen of him," said this witness. James Cook noted this sudden withdrawal. He had turned to see which cowhand fired the threatening shot. "When I looked toward the place where Baca had been standing," said the cowboy leader, "he was gone." William French observed Baca emerge "hastily" from the courtroom, as he pulled "his hat down over his eyes." The deputy entered a house a short distance down the road in Middle Plaza. Deputy Baca later explained that he sought sanctuary from the threatening mob. At his trial, Baca led the court to believe that his conversation with Wilson precipitated the lawman's retreat. When Baca drew his pistol and informed Wilson that he "did not want to talk to him either. . . .then I went out in the direction of Jeronimo's [Armijo's] house." In his 1924 political pamphlet, the former officer referred to the anonymous cowhand's pistol shot. Afterwards, "I drew my guns and backed up to a picket house called a *jacal*, belonging to . . . Geronimo Armijo." This mysterious behavior of the deputy did not concern James Cook for long. When he learned of the release of Charles McCarthy, the WS rancher gathered his crew and began to depart Upper Plaza.[40]

While the trial of Charles McCarthy was under way, William French and his friends were seated on the ground nearby enjoying a mumblety-peg game. "A few stragglers" from Milligan's saloon soon joined this "foreign contingent," as they flipped open pocket knives. Among the onlookers was William B. (Bert) Hearne, a John B. Slaughter hand. Hearne was evidently drunk and in a prankish mood. He decided "to test the nerves of the tenderfoot from abroad," according to William French, who wrote:

> After watching us for a few moments one of them [spectators], whose name was [William] Hern, discharged a Winchester [rifle] . . . into the ground within two or three inches of my feet. The bullet tore a great gash in the ground. . . . I took no notice of it. . . . the crowd dispersed, and . . . disappeared [back] into Mr. Milligan's Hall of Entertainment.

Hearne was to play an unfortunate part in subsequent events that day. As James Cook led his group out of town, some of French's men joined the cavalcade. French remained behind at the request of Dan Milligan, who offered him a farewell drink.[41]

The friends of Young Parham were determined to see Deputy Sheriff Baca pay for the cowhand's death. William W. Wilson, the cattlemen's justice of the peace, issued an arrest warrant and commissioned several cowboys as deputy constables. These ad hoc lawmen included Jerome Wadsworth, William B. Hearne and others. French recalled that Hearne and two other men approached him as he was leaving the grog shop:

> They asked me if I had seen where Mr. Baca went when he came out of the court-room. I pointed out the cabin [of Geronimo Armijo] and was preparing to mount when they told me they had authority from the presiding justice to arrest Mr. Baca. The ostensible reason was the shooting of the man [Parham] at the time of McCarthy's arrest. They said it was only just that he should be made to answer according to law.

The Englishman agreed to join Hearne, now evidently a deputy constable, and empowered to make the arrest. "Let's go ahead and arrest him," said French, who, with Hearne and two others, "walked down to the cabin" where Deputy Sheriff Baca had taken sanctuary. James Wadsworth gave a different reason for the search for Baca. This cowboy informed the court during Baca's subsequent trial that the lawman still had Charles McCarthy's pistol. The latter desired it before he departed town.[42]

The Geronimo Armijo house in Middle Plaza became the focus of the ongoing contest between cowboys and lawman. William French observed firsthand the next outbreak of violence as he and Hearne approached the house:

> Hern, who had taken the lead, walked up to the door and I followed close behind him. He knocked, asking if there was anyone there. Receiving no reply, he kicked the door violently, demanding admittance. The reply [of Baca] was decisive. It came in the form of a bullet

> through the door, which took him [Hearne] in the abdomen.

The cowhand "swore a marvellous oath" and crumpled into French's arms. James Wadsworth, who was also present, saw the mortally wounded man stagger backward, climb over a fence, and collapse on the ground. Friends took him to Milligan's bar and eventually to Joe Armstrong's house some two miles above Apache Creek on the road to Socorro. Armstrong was Slaughter's trail boss. Hearne died there.[43]

William French's account of this shooting has remained the standard one for many years. Jerome Wadsworth, who was one of the primary representatives of the cattlemen, also provided an eyewitness report at the trial of Elfego Baca. The cowboys, not knowing for certain if Baca was in the Armijo house, obtained keys to a padlock on the door:

> I got the keys to his [Armijo's] house, and with several others went there; one of the men said the door was not locked and Burt Hurn [Hearne] tried to open it; as he pushed on the door two shots were fired by someone in the house and Burt staggered back and said, "Boys I'm killed."[44]

Elfego Baca later filled in some details of his movement to the Armijo house. He recalled that Geronimo's son, Molo, was on top of the residence shucking corn as the deputy hurried toward the house. Baca ordered the boy off the roof "in a hurry" while the peace officer also "put the lady and [other] children out." In his trial, Baca provided a fuller explanation of his actions:

> I watched to see if anyone was following me [from the courtroom]; I entered the house and the woman [Josefa Armijo] locked the door and went away, I don't know where; I heard several men round the house; I heard them talk, and they wanted to kill me; one of them said that it was just a padlock that fastened the door, and they had better go and get a key; they went away and returned in a few minutes; and pushed the door; they

> again went around the house; one of them said "this door is not locked"; he shoved the door at one of the middle rooms; the others were trying to unlock the door; I remained where I was; they pushed on the door but did not open it; when they did not open the door, they all said, "let us fire"; they commenced firing through all the doors, and I fired a few shots through the windows, then they pushed the door again, and I fired two shots through the door.

Baca wrote in his political pamphlet in the 1920s that he saw Hearne dismount from his horse and hurry toward the cabin, exclaiming, "I'll get the little Mexican out of there." Baca then shot at him with both guns at the same time "through the cracks in the door." In subsequent testimony, Baca added that there were ten or eleven in the mob and that "some had rifles and all had pistols." They "said they would get me out [forcibly]," the deputy volunteered.[45]

Upon cross examination, the former deputy altered his recollections of this encounter:

> There was only one door and one window in the [portion of the] house where I was; they came up to the house from an easterly direction; they rode around the house; [I] did fire two shots through the door when one of them said he would get me out; no shots were fired previous[ly]; the men came to the door only once; some one of them made a proposition to get some keys and get into the house; they tried to open the door when they came back; they were gone about four or five minutes; some were on foot and others on horseback; after the man said that they would get me out they commenced shooting.[46]

The stockmen's testimony naturally disagreed with Elfego Baca about the circumstances around the house. On cross examination, Jerome Wadsworth said:

> There were about eight or nine men with us; we did not

> go into the house; did not see who was inside; . . .after the two shots were fired, several others were heard in the rear of the house; did not know of any shots being fired on the [house ?]; the men were all around, did not furnish [Charles] McCarthy with any arms; the men had their pistols in their scabbards; four or five of them had rifles; . . .defendant had two 45's [revolvers] at the time he left the justice of the peace's office.

O. B. Bishop, another of the cowboy brigade, admitted that "someone pushed on the door" of the Armijo house, and "two shots were fired from inside the house." However, "nothing was said from inside the house" in warning before the shots.[47]

Other members of the search party took the same position. A. M. Loftiss denied that the cowboy contingent "said anything about killing [the] defendant." Loftiss averred that he heard "every word that was spoken" and believed that he "would probably have heard it if anything had been said." He admitted that the mob made "lots of loud talk," but that the searchers had concluded that Baca had fled the house since the lawman had made no reply to their approach. Loftiss said that no member of the cattlemen's group "went around the house till after [Baca's] shots were fired." O. B. Bishop also "heard conversation" among the herders but he "did not hear anyone say that they would kill the defendant." Charles McCarthy, whose drunken antics had set off this confrontation, testified that he heard the mob's utterances, none of which were "threats" to the deputy's life. Montague Stevens, who was in the vicinity but not an eyewitness, later declared that Baca "opened up on them without a word." Stevens compressed the two separate shootings—of Parham and Hearne—into one incident in his account.[48]

Elfego Baca's defense counsel later adopted the position that the cattlemen's congregation threatened his client's life. The cowboy witnesses attempted to discredit this position and held that the deputy overreacted. Some question was raised about the manner in which Baca left the justice's office and whether he acted as though his life were in danger. The stockmen declared that Baca did not have his weapons drawn and that he did not say anything to lead anyone to believe he was taking refuge at the Armijo house to save his life. Jerome Wadsworth stated that "I did not see him [Baca] draw a pistol on anybody" as he departed the courtroom. Evidently, the defense attempted to demonstrate that Wadsworth and the cattlemen's committee violated the written agreement not to molest Baca and his guards. This breach of faith led the deputy sheriff to take refuge. Under cross examination, Wadsworth protested that he "Did not violate the contract."[49]

The shooting of William Hearne aroused the cowboys to greater anger. Once again, the cattle interests went to their justice of the peace, William Wilson, for an arrest warrant. He complied with a handwritten document dated 1 November:

> You ar[e] commanded to go and arest [*sic*] the person of A. Baca eney whare [*sic*] you may find him in Socorro County and take him or bring him to this or some other justice of the peace of Socorro county to answer to a charge of murder of the person of W. B. Hearne on the 30th day of October 1884.[50]

Now clothed with official colors, the cowboys prepared to lay siege on Deputy Sheriff Baca's place of refuge. This episode remains the most widely publicized aspect of "the Mexican war." Baca later wrote that "The court evidence shows that over four thousand shots [elsewhere he said only 400] were fired at me within thirty-six hours." Kyle Crichton, Baca's biographer, avers that 367 bullet holes were found in a single door and that every furnishing in the house was destroyed. He adds that one portion of the house literally collapsed under gunfire. Through this withering fire, the gutsy deputy held his ground without a scratch. One version declares that Baca survived because the sunken floor of the Armijo house enabled him to take refuge below ground. Montague Stevens remarked that Baca fell "flat on [the] floor." Abe B. Baca declared Elfego "dug himself a foxhole and piled the dirt around him." Legend also says that providence intervened. The evidence was the presence of a statue of Santa Ana, which was the only accoutrement of the house untouched by rifle fire. The casualty figures for this siege were also greatly exaggerated. From the one man—William Hearne—killed, Baca magnified the figure to four killed and eight wounded. The *Black Range*, the first newspaper to report, said five men died and a "big killing" was feared, though Hearne was actually the only casualty.[51]

While the facts of this siege are by no means clear, some points do emerge more distinctly. The besieging force did not maintain a constant fire upon the Armijo house, nor did the cowboys fire 4,000 rounds into the fragile building, as Baca later asserted. Montague Stevens reportedly scoffed at this exaggeration years later and declared that the cattlemen's force did not possess that amount of ammunition. The efforts of the cowboys to dislodge Baca were sporadic at best. Baca had time to relax. He recalled that "I found some beef and made beef stew, coffee and tortillas." James Cook's party heard the shooting—the gunfire that led to Hearne's death—as the horsemen were leaving the plaza. Cook later wrote that he feared the growing number of Hispanos, who gathered on nearby hillsides, had descended upon the Texans. The WS general manager led his followers pell mell into Middle Plaza and blundered into Deputy Baca's pistol range. One bullet narrowly missed Charles (Old Charlie) Moore and another shot tore mud from an adobe wall near Cook's head. Moore had stopped to gather up the reins of French's strayed horse and was leading it to safety. French ran to the assistance of Moore and lost his hat in the street. In the meantime, Moore had received a bullet through his "tall, peaked hat." Although Baca had two pistols, it is doubtful that he possessed more than a few rounds of ammunition or a belt of cartridges at best. Nevertheless, "Excitement now ran high," recalled Cook, who found the friends of the dying cowhand, William Hearne, dressing his wound in the rear of Dan Milligan's saloon.[52]

The young hothead lingered only a short time. Englishman Alfred Hardcastle, who had also witnessed this shooting, saw Hearne expire in the rear of Milligan's store. Hardcastle then played an unusual part in the coroner's inquest:

> I shall never forget it, . . .I was elected foreman of the jury, and sat on the end of the bench, which, with sundry boxes and flour sacks, constituted the jury box. But—and this I believe is the unique part—I was also called as the principal witness!

Upon completion of his testimony, Hardcastle returned to the foreman's seat. According to this foreign visitor, the coroner's jury found Elfego Baca guilty of murder in the first degree and sentence him to death. This was "a climax hardly to be expected at an inquest!" Hardcastle rightly concluded, since such bodies did not possess the authority to impose penalties.[53]

Back at the besieged *jacal*, James Cook had again assumed the role of spokesman. He feared that more bloodshed would result if the herders attempted to drive Deputy Sheriff Baca from his refuge. While this gathering may have possessed the official color of a constable or deputy sheriff's posse, neither Cook nor William French emphasized this formal status. "At Cook's suggestion some attempt was made to parley," wrote William French, but "All we got was more shots" from Deputy Baca. Ed Erway, another WS employee, now attempted to sneak up to the house, only to be spied and "forced to retreat." Whether this attempt inspired the legend that one besieger girded himself in a cast iron stove door and charged the house is not known. French and others fired at "every nook and cranny" of the picket-house. "How he escaped the numerous bullets . . . was a mystery to us," concluded French. Consultation with Deputy Sheriff Bechtol failed to arouse his sense of duty. French and Charles Moore found him again asleep at Milligan's. French and other members of the siege party—apparently only eight or ten men participated actively—posted sentries for the approaching night, 30/31 October 1884. Evidently, French took his duties as posseman seriously. He remained awake all night and walked patrol to ensure that the guards did not fall asleep. He finally went to sleep in Milligan's back room about 5 a. m. the thirty-first. He arose about mid- morning to breakfast with a friend, John Cox, the former cavalry sergeant.[54]

The besieging force continued its work in earnest on the thirty-first. Montague Stevens reported that "others came in" and that this new contingent "shot [into] the cabin some more." The cowboys stretched blankets between nearby houses in order to mask their movements. Messengers rode to Cooney mining camp, some twenty miles south of Frisco Plaza, for dynamite with which to destroy the Armijo house. French reported that they also threw burning logs upon the roof "but the darn thing was made of dirt about a foot thick and refused to ignite." One newspaper reported erroneously that the torches worked and forced Baca out. A legend continues to circulate, reinforced by Kyle Crichton's biography of Baca, that the cowboys did employ dynamite against the deputy's sanctuary. This is apparently in error, although the details of these incidents could possibly have been covered in the day of trial testimony not reported by the *Albuquerque Evening Democrat*.[55]

In the meantime, the crowd of Hispanos continued to grow on the hillsides surrounding the village. Although they did not betray any intention of joining in the battle, the stockmen worried. French heard a report that these partisans of Deputy Baca planned to descend upon the besiegers. The cowboys fired a few shots in the direction of the spectators. French admitted that they learned later that these onlookers were part of a delegation destined for Socorro, the county seat. They wanted to alert Sheriff Pedro Simpson to his subordinate's dilemma. By late afternoon of the thirty-first, says French, the "army" of cowboy besiegers began to grow "grumpy" and "drowsy." Having lost sleep and consumed too much of "Mr. Milligan's forty rod whiskey," they lacked the necessary resolve to carry out their threat to expel the lawman from his fortress.[56]

James H. Cook was in an awkward position. He resented being "crowded" into the position of spokesman and regarded many of his followers as a mere mob:

> A number of my English friends were with me at the Plaza, also my brother [Jack F. Cook]. I told them that I considered the Americans . . . neither more nor less than a mob. Baca, I was informed, was a county officer, and the law was on his side. I felt that although he may have overdone his duty, the best thing possible for all was not to kill him, but to secure him and get him to the county seat at Socorro.

Apparently these "English friends" were Harold C. Wilson, owner of the WS ranch (and not related to the other Wilsons), French, Montague Stevens, Alfred Hardcastle, and others.[57]

Just when James Cook's task appeared hopeless, good fortune rode his way late on the afternoon of 31 October. Deputy Sheriff Frank Rose [mistakenly called Ross in most accounts], Francisquito Naranjo, and an undentified third man comprised the official party from Socorro. Naranjo, whom Baca regarded as "a good friend," had summoned these authorities. Rose refused to take immediate command of the situation, although he represented Sheriff Pedro Simpson. Presumably, Rose did not desire to interfere with Deputy Dan Bechtol's position until he assessed the situation. Cook expressed disappointment at this delay, rightly fearing more bloodshed. The cowman urged Rose to approach his beleaguered colleague immediately. Deputy Sheriff Bechtol chose to arouse himself at this point. He emerged from Milligan's bar, recalled French, "reciting what he had not done to enforce respect for the law." When Rose refused to listen, the humiliated deputy sheriff retired to the saloon. Fortunately, Cook persuaded a Hispano—the messenger, Naranjo—to approach Elfego Baca with a proposition. "If Baca were alive and would give himself up," said Cook, "I would be responsible to them [the Hispanic community] for his life until he could be taken to the county seat." Naranjo presented this proposal and reassured Baca that the inhabitants of the community knew Cook as a property owner and that he "could not afford to lie" and continue to reside in the area.[58]

To the great surprise of the onlookers, Baca responded positively. He did not mention the mediary but recalled talking to Cook and Rose. Baca stipulated that he would emerge from his bastion only when the cowboy element withdrew. He would submit to arrest only to Deputy Rose, but "I will not surrender my guns." The deputy insisted upon protection for the trip to Socorro, the county seat. Cook promised an escort of six cowboys. With these preliminaries concluded, Baca suddenly appeared. Said Cook:

> Suddenly Baca sprang out of the jacal through a small window . . . .He had a six-shooter in each hand and was clad only in his underclothes. As he came towards me, many of the Mexicans on the hills yelled for him to run to them. Luckily he did not attempt to do so, for many rifles in the hands of the best shots [cowboys] in New Mexico were trained upon him.[59]

French confirms this inglorious appearance "through a little window in the gable end of the house." The Englishman and others of the cowboy party had withdrawn in order to comply with Baca's terms of surrender. To everyone's surprise the lawman emerged near French's new position:

> He was like a wild animal, stripped to his shirt, with a revolver in each hand, looking suspiciously on every side of him, as if fearing treachery. I [French] withdrew behind my shelter as he came in sight, and after satisfying himself that no one was lying in wait for him he went up to Mr. Rose, who disarmed him.

Kyle Crichton, Baca's biographer, declared that his subject "denies vehemently" the report that he surrendered in underclothes. Certainly, Baca had good cause to suspect the possibility of a lynch mob. He recalled later that the terrible fate of Joel Fowler, a recent victim of the Socorro "stranglers," persuaded Baca "to be careful of his friendships." Many personal friends of the two dead men, Parham and Hearne, were present at his surrender to Deputy Rose. Nor did this young prisoner know Frank Rose well enough to have absolute faith in him.[60]

This spectacular standoff between the lone Hispano policeman and the cattlemen ended after some twenty-four hours (Baca maintained that at least thirty-six hours passed) but the tension continued into the next day, 1 November. Justice of the Peace Wilson formally issued the warrant for Baca on that day. James Cook recalled that some expressed a desire to lynch Baca in spite of the agreement, but the WS general manager counselled letting the law take its course. As Cook explained to his associates, he had pledged his word and any violation would result in "a fine little race war." Alfred Hardcastle asserted many years later that, indeed, some cowboys plotted to seize Elfego Baca at a place called Point of Rocks near the headwaters of the Tularosa River; but they became confused as to which group would carry out this grim assignment and failed to intercept Deputy Rose's party. Whatever the bluster of the Texan element, the Hispanos still outnumbered the stockmen in western Socorro County. However unpleasant the thought, the warlike cowboys would have to learn to live with (and eventually marry into) the native population.[61]

Deputy Sheriff Rose continued to fret about the safety of his prisoner as long as they remained in Frisco Plaza. In the absence of a secure jail—Baca had housed McCarthy in a private residence—Rose employed a shrewd substitute. When Deputy Sheriff Bechtol ceremonially turned Baca over to Rose, the latter officer asked William French's WS party to guard Baca the night of 31 October/1 November 1884. This component of the cattlemen's interests lacked the personal involvement of the Slaughter cowboys. The WS herders took Elfego Baca to Milligan's saloon—apparently the sole mecca in the area—and permitted him food and a bath. When subsequently asked about this bit of irony—eating with French and others who had just tried to kill him—Elfego had little to say. "I ate dinner with some men afterward," he said, "but I don't remember who they were." James Cook says that the deputy's Prince Albert coat was found in the Armijo cabin and returned to him. Baca later scoffed that he did not own such a garment. This story still remains inseparable from the legend of Baca's battle with the cowboys and probably arises from the fact that he later enjoyed dapper dress.[62]

The official party began the journey to Socorro on 1 November. This entourage included Rose, Baca, A. M. Loftiss as driver of the buckboard, and an escort of six cowboys. Elfego Baca continued to worry for his life. William Hearne's friends were still mourning his death. At his trial some months later, Baca recalled that "on the way to Socorro we overtook a team and wagon containing a coffin; but [I] did not ask who was in the coffin for the reason that I thought I might be in one myself soon." Furthermore, he distrusted the six-man escort. He demanded that they ride "at least thirty long paces . . . ahead" of the buckboard. The trip proved uneventful. Upon arrival in the county seat, on or about 4 November, Deputy Sheriff Frank Rose took his prisoner before Justice of the Peace W. E. Kelly, who bound Baca over for action of the grand jury.[63]

Although the residents of western Socorro County had narrowly averted a very costly "war," the cattle interests continued their political crusade against Sheriff Pedro A. Simpson. The editor of the Chloride *Black Range*, which had published an early

Baca was placed in the jail in the rear of the newly constructed Socorro County courthouse in 1884. (Photo by J.R. Riddle, Museum of New Mexico)

and very slanted version of the clash between Simpson's deputy and the cowboys, was a leader in the effort to discredit the sheriff. Among other offenses, the *Black Range* accused him of failing to account for taxes collected and of helping his political cronies obtain "a pull at the public bottle through the sheriff's office." These ardent stockmen succeeded in electing a fellow cattleman, Charles T. Russell, to this important office just a week after the battle at Frisco Plaza. Elfego Baca's defiance of the herders apparently emboldened the villagers. Deputy Sheriff Pedro Sarracino of Lower Plaza took heart and began to arrest reckless horsemen. Jefferson Davis Milton, a cattle detective and deputy of the new Socorro County sheriff, ran afoul of Sarracino shortly after the shootout at Middle Plaza. Sarracino arrested Milton for horse theft and took him before an Hispano justice of the peace, possibly Lopez. Milton soon concluded the trial proceedings were "a travesty on justice." He found a pretext to be momentarily excused. He and his friends fled to John B. Slaughter's ranch, which apparently continued to be a cowboy rallying point. While Milton's memory cannot always be relied upon, he alleged that some Hispanos—still chafing over the Baca episode—ambushed him and another cowboy on the Upper Gila River. Milton was wounded, but he and his friend managed to kill three ambushers. When Sheriff Charles Russell received word of this mysterious shooting, he suggested that Deputy Milton investigate. The subordinate assured him that there was no truth in this report. Contemporary newspapers did not report such an incident. However, Jeff Milton's hazy recollections of this tense era in western Socorro County reflect the continuation of stockmen's hostility.[64]

Elfego Baca's ordeal was not over, since the cattle interests were intent upon pressing their case against him. They insisted that Baca and his posse should pay for the deaths of Young Parham and William B. Hearne. The victory of Charles T. Russell, the former Texan, in the shrievalty race added strength to their cause. The incumbent, Pedro A. Simpson—Baca's superior—would turn over the reins of office on 1 January 1885. Whether Simpson revoked Elfego Baca's commission after the Frisco Plaza shooting is not clear. The deputy lost his effectiveness when legal charges were filed against him. In any event, all deputyships ended with the change over in the office of chief county lawman.[65]

A Socorro County grand jury indicted Baca for murder at the spring 1885 session of district court. Elfego Baca obtained a change of venue to Bernalillo County, where he could be assured an Hispano jury. The newly elected sheriff in Albuquerque was Santiago Baca. Whether the two Bacas were related is not clear, although the sheriff deputized Elfego after his trial. At the trial, which occurred in May 1885, his counsel successfully argued self defense. Baca was acquitted. The former deputy sheriff's enemies remained unconvinced. A second grand jury indicted him and some members of his Frisco Plaza posse at the fall 1885 term of Socorro court. Again, he was acquitted. The Anglo press grumbled that these trials were "farces," since the juries always consisted of Hispanos, and characterized Baca as "the Socorro murderer." The Chloride *Black Range* went so far as to confuse Elfego Baca with Enofre Baca who had callously murdered an

Anglo newspaper editor in Socorro in 1880. Such adverse publicity was calculated to blacken the name of the former deputy sheriff.[66]

The miraculous survival of Elfego Baca in the rencontre at Frisco Plaza and his refusal to be bullied had the effect of stiffening the resolve of his countrymen. He had demonstrated to the new arrivals that the native New Mexicans upheld the rule of law and that they were just as adept with weapons as the cowboys. As Baca's obituary later noted, his exploit at Frisco Plaza was "a living denial of jibes at Spanish-Americans' ineptitude with firearms." While much exaggeration arose about this shootout, such distortions do not rule out a degree of bravery, even foolhardiness on the part of Elfego Baca. The intentions of the cattle element—Texan and otherwise—were not at all clear. Some, such as James Cook, objected to the senseless and roughshod practices of the herders. Probably not all cowhands intended mayhem during their drunken sprees in Frisco Plaza, but their rampages often went to brutal excess. Charles McCarthy's binge revealed such dangers. The combination of ethnic enmity and frequent recourse to Dan Milligan's saloon was calculated to lead to bloodshed. Deputy Sheriff Elfego Baca's sudden appearance introduced an unknown quantity. His defiance of the cowboys impressed even the deputy's enemies. The threat of further bloodshed pushed the moderate element among the stockmen to the front, and compromise (sometimes written) resulted. This sane solution perhaps demonstrated the emergence of healthier attitudes in both communities and set a precedent for future accommodations. But the most immediate outcome seemed to be victory for Elfego Baca and his followers. "It might seem the honours went to Baca," concluded William French humorously, "unless one heard our own deputy, Dan [Bechtol], swell up and relate what he and his posse had done."[67]

CHAPTER THREE

DISCREET SURVEILLANCE

The confrontation at Frisco Plaza and the subsequent trial of Elfego Baca made him a local celebrity among the Hispanic population. At the same time, the hostility of the growing cattle interests in Socorro County may have influenced him to relocate. Baca moved to Albuquerque and soon became an active member of the law enforcement community. Santiago Baca, Bernalillo County Sheriff in 1885-86, deputized the controversial young man. This commission probably raised some eyebrows, but the chief county lawman may have believed such official coloring was necessary to protect Elfego Baca from malicious prosecution. It does not appear that the two men were related. Like Elfego Baca, Santiago Baca represented the new generation of Hispanos who consciously competed in the world of the American interlopers. Santiago Baca had opened a business in New Town, Albuquerque, in the midst of these new arrivals. He joined civic groups and participated wholeheartedly in the heated politics of that day. Elfego Baca retained his deputy's badge under Santiago Baca's successors, through 1888. The Republican United States marshal for New Mexico, Trinidad Romero, also awarded this aspiring young lawman a concurrent deputy's commission for 1887-88. Elfego also served as a sergeant in the local militia company.[68]

On 13 August 1885 Elfego Baca married Francisca Pohmer, daughter of German-born Joseph Pohmer, an Albuquerque baker and merchant. He later enjoyed telling the story about their first meeting and courtship. Baca was walking down an Albuquerque street during a recess in his trial when he encountered the striking sixteen-year-old maiden. He vowed to make her his bride. Elfego and Francisca raised six children: Alfredo A., Josefina, Sofia, George, Juanita, and Lucila.[69]

Elfego Baca continued to agitate on behalf of the Hispanos in spite of his narrow escape at Frisco Plaza. During a visit to Socorro, he reportedly attended the trial of a fellow Hispano, who was charged with the death of an Anglo cowboy. Baca's older brother, Abdenago, was a member of the jury. When the panel, which included a majority of Spanish-Americans, refused to indict the accused, the district attorney accused Abdenago of steering the jury to this irresponsible act. The attorney demanded that the judge remove the elder Baca. When the bench complied, Elfego Baca jumped to his feet in the audience, shook his fist at the astonished judge, and shouted, "You stupid, corrupt, immoral so and so!" The judge ordered the sheriff to jail "this upstart," but the lawman and his deputies, "foreseeing and forestalling an encounter with Elfego," quickly disappeared. According to this account, the man on the bench was soon removed because of "immoral behavior." While this story is no doubt exaggerated, it may contain a kernel of truth and reflected the emergence of the legend of Elfego Baca. Certainly, this brash and assertive young man was capable of creating such a scene in a frontier courtroom.[70]

Elfego Baca clashed with members of the Anglo community on many occasions. In September 1886, he and Sheriff Santiago Baca quarreled with an Albuquerque city policeman, E. D. Henry. The newspapers, also owned by Anglos, reported that these Bernalillo County officers assaulted Henry and that friends and supporters rushed to the aid of each side. This incident "almost provoked a race riot," said one journalist. The two Bacas were arrested but apparently released. A few weeks later, these quarrelsome lawmen joined forces to pursue Charlie Ross and John "Kid" Johnson and one Hardy, three hard cases who murdered City Marshal Robert McGuire and Policeman Henry, the officer with whom Baca had feuded earlier. Ross was eventually arrested after an attempt to rob a train on the Atlantic and Pacific Railroad in the following January; however, he escaped the Albuquerque jail and was not recaptured. Hardy was killed. The eventual fate of Johnson is not known.[71]

Trouble seemed to accompany Elfego Baca in his youthful days. On 9 September 1889, he had another rencontre with an Albuquerque lawman. Although Elfego Baca was no longer on the sheriff's force, Juan Baca, a deputy and concurrent city policeman, stabbed the former lawman and inflicted "a dangerous cut" below the ribs. The *Albuquerque Morning Democrat* admitted that "a bitter enmity" existed between the two men. (They were not related.) Deputy Sheriff Juan Baca realized that he had committed an indiscreet act and quickly pleaded guilty to assault and battery, hoping to avoid a more aggravated charge. The outcome of this case is unclear, although Elfego later attributed this, and other such personal encounters, to "political peregrinations."[72]

Like the majority of New Mexico Hispanos, Elfego Baca belonged to the Republican Party and demonstrated a fervent interest in politics and public office all of his life. Although Baca denied that his mission to San Francisco Plaza in October 1884, which set off his future public career, was to make speeches for Sheriff Pedro Simpson, this purpose can not be ruled out completely. In 1888 the budding politician returned briefly to Socorro to campaign on behalf of the Republican candidate for sheriff. Although Baca's fight with the cowboys had taken place four years earlier, the local GOP used the memory of this enounter to try to discredit R. J. Bishop, the Democratic candidate. Baca was accused by Bishop of deliberately spreading the story that he "was one of a party who made an assault upon him at Frisco, . . . and . . . [of being] a member of the grand jury that found indictments against him." The angry candidate expressed dismay at such a low tactic and protested that he "always refrained from [attacking] personalities." In a published reply to such misinformation, Bishop reminded readers that "I was not in the territory at that time, nor was I a member of the grand jury." Clarence A. Robinson, a popular Socorran, won this shrieval election. Elfego had apparently confused this Bishop with O. B. Bishop, who had testified against him in 1885.[73]

No stigma was attached to such political tactics in that day, and Elfego Baca's popularity continued to grow. Not only was he ambitious but he was willing to work. In October 1893 he received an appointment as deputy county clerk of Socorro County. This post had become vacant upon the death of the incumbent, Estanislao Pino. In November Baca won the clerkship, an indication that the old animosity toward him among some citizens was moderating. The fact that his brother Abe held positions of public trust in the county no doubt helped paved the way for the younger sibling. Like most local officials, the clerk earned his income from fees for services rendered to private citizens. Elfego later boasted that he refused to charge fees in November and December of each year, in order to permit "the poor people" of his county to obtain his services free of charge. He held this important county post from 1894 through 1897.[74]

The young man had begun to read law at an early age, possibly soon after returning from Topeka, Kansas, in 1881. His legal education took on new meaning when he acquired family responsibilities. He studied in the Socorro office of Humphrey B. Hamilton, a former Missourian. Such training provided "scant preparation," as he later admitted to fellow attorney William A. Keleher. But he read a sufficient amount from a few standard books, including William Blackstone's *Commentaries on the Laws of England*. As early as 1892, Baca was reported practicing law, although he was not formally admitted to the New Mexico Bar until July 1895. This novice attorney apparently demonstrated some promise, since Andreius A. Freeman, a former territorial supreme court justice, admitted him into partnership. As Baca said through his biographer, Kyle Crichton, "the firm had a standing of high rank from the start." His legal career could not have begun more auspiciously, and he maintained an office in either Socorro or Albuquerque—he alternated residences frequently—for the remainder of his long life. In 1902 Baca opened a branch office in El Paso, although his home base remained in Socorro. In April 1905, the *Las Cruces Citizen* noted that he had just vacated his quarters in the Chambon Building on Court Street in Socorro. On the following day, John Fullerton, captain of the newly established Mounted Police, occupied this suite.[75]

While Elfego Baca achieved political and economic success, he could not avoid personal difficulties. In April 1896, he got into a fight with W. E. Martin, another Socorran. The *Rio Grande Republican* reported that Baca became drunk on the twenty- fourth and shot at the victim. While the gunman's rounds failed to hit the target, this journalist went out of his way to point out that Elfego Baca was the Socorro County clerk, leaving the impression that this was very unofficer-like behavior. In the following month, the case of the *Territory v. Elfego Baca*, charged with assault to kill, came before the district court. Although the details are unclear, Baca's defense attorney filed for a dismissal. He cited a technicality—the foreman of the grand jury was also the postmaster—thus constituting a conflict of interest. The final disposition of the case is not known.[76]

Baca continued to maintain a busy presence in Socorro County politics, winning and losing at various times. He lost bids for the county collectorship and, in 1900, the judgeship of the fifth judicial district. However, for 1900-1901 he won election to the school superintendency, a position of great importance and sensitivity. The New Mexico Public School System was of recent origin, having been instituted in 1891, after a long and bitter struggle between the growing Anglo minority and the Hispanos who were accustomed to the Catholic Church's educational system. His wife, Francisca, also possessed an interest in education, having attended the first class at the Albuquerque Academy in 1879. Baca's ties with both Anglo and Hispano communities may have enabled him to modulate successfully between the rival groups. Baca attempted to encourage attendance by awarding prizes for good attendance, a doll for girls and a medal for boys. He averred that such incentives "did a lot of good" and encouraged the pupils to study. Since his district included all of Socorro County, the school superintendent had a great responsibility. When Bessie Cavanaugh, one of his former teachers, wrote Elfego Baca many years later, he confessed that it was "impossible for me to remember all the school teachers in Socorro County." In 1903 residents of Socorro selected Baca for the mayor's office.[77]

Although a busy man, Elfego Baca continued to serve as a deputy sheriff when called upon. Indeed, he may have carried a badge regularly, but served only at the behest of the Socorro County sheriff. In May 1895, Baca participated in the purusit of

Jose Chavez y Chavez, a veteran tough who had a criminal record as early as the Lincoln County War. At this time, Chavez was a member of the Vicente Silva band which preyed upon San Miguel County. As a deputy to Sheriff Holm O. Bursum, Baca trailed Chavez into the far western precincts of Socorro County and made the arrest. Deputy Baca trailed another accused murderer, Jose Garcia, into present-day Sandoval County, in northern New Mexico. Baca took along a young Hispanic, Alfredo Montoya, who knew the back trails of the sheep ranges where Garcia had taken refuge. Using the trailing skills of Montoya and donning a disguise as a black man, Baca successfully snared the fugitive.[78]

The possession of such manhunting skills may have persuaded Elfego Baca to open a detective agency. Private sleuthing had become common in late 1800s, since many propertied Americans believed that public law enforcement agencies were unable to curb the growing crime rate. The economy-minded Baca distributed business cards which read "Attorney at Law" and on the reverse, "Private Detective, Discrete Surveillance Done." Baca was sufficiently aware that the simultaneous practice of both enterprises could expose him to accusations of unprofessional conduct. William A. Keleher, a fellow attorney and occasional confidant, recalled that Baca was "Anxious to observe the niceties of the legal profession." Although "headstrong" and a "determined man," said Keleher, Baca took the time to ask him about "ethical problems" that arose as he attempted to carry on the two professions.[79]

Just how successful Baca's detective business was is difficult to say. In July 1893, the *Daily New Mexican* observed him in Santa Fe in search of an accused murderer. Baca also garnered some information about an attempted assassination in the territorial capital in 1891. The goal of the assassins was either Thomas B. Catron or Joseph Ancheta, both influential politicians. The gunmen's bullets hit and seriously wounded the latter, but may have been intended for the former. Elfego Baca informed the authorities that he had received a tip from a relative who had overheard the assassins (apparently legislators) concocting their plot against Ancheta. Ancheta survived but never regained his health and the hit men were never found.[80]

Elfego Baca also took a keen interest in another controversial assassination. In February 1896, unknown assailants murdered lawyer Albert Jennings Fountain and his eight-year- old son, Henry, in the White Sands near Las Cruces. While Fountain had made many enemies in his controversial public and legal life, New Mexicans were incensed, especially at the murder of the child. Governor William Thornton, an active crusader for law and order, obtained a $20,000 appropriation with which to offer a reward and press the investigation. He also sought a man with criminal-fighting credentials to head the search. Although Elfego Baca regarded himself as the man of the hour, Governor Thornton selected the more noted former lawman, Pat Garrett, the killer of Billy the Kid. In a somewhat arbitrary measure, the governor maneuvered out the incumbent sheriff of Doña Ana County—the site of the murders—and appointed Garrett. According to writer Leon Metz, Baca complained "that Governor Thornton had chosen the wrong man to solve the Fountain mystery." Metz believes that Thornton rightly chose Pat Garrett because he "was not the braggart that Baca was." Thornton also employed the Pinkerton National Detective Agency to assist Garrett.[81]

This slight did not dissuade Elfego Baca from offering his services. Not only did he believe that he possessed better entrees into the New Mexico underworld than Pat Garrett, but Baca and Fountain were friends and fellow Republicans. On the day that Fountain and his son had departed Lincoln, Elfego had arranged to travel with them to Las Cruces, and then by train to Socorro. Unfortunately, Baca was detained by the sudden appearance of a prospective client. In any event, Baca sought evidence on his own and apparently concluded that a Socorro County badman may have been involved. On 19 April 1896, Pinkerton Operative J. C. Fraser visited the New Mexico gumshoe, who "told me that Maxammeano Greago [Maximiano Griego, informant] would be here [in Socorro] this evening." This clue failed to lead to worthwhile results, and the Pinkerton man soon concluded that Elfego Baca was merely a "frontier confidence man."[82]

These setbacks failed to discourage the private detective. In November 1898, Grant Gillett, a wealthy cattle raiser and speculator in Abilene, Kansas, ran afoul of the law and took refuge in

Mexico. Gillett, who reportedly owned 200,000 head of livestock, was accused of negotiating multiple mortgages on his herd. Attachment suits were levied against him for $40,000. This was just the beginning of his problems and prompted an extended stay of several years in Mexico. His debts soon amounted to one and one-half million dollars. Elfego Baca later claimed that Gillett's creditors placed a $50,000 reward on the fugitive's head, although newspaper reports do not mention any such head money. James H. Arnold, a business associate of Gillett, believed that he merely became over-extended, began to "rob Peter to pay Paul," and soon could satisfy no creditors. "I do not think he was guilty of anything more than this," said Arnold. In early 1899, Arnold shuttled between Chihuahua and Kansas with C. R. Troxel, Gillett's attorney, in a futile effort to arrange a compromise settlement with Gillett's creditors. Gillett's victims decided to wait out the speculator, who, in the meantime, languished in exile in the southern republic. By March the Gillett case had received so much publicity that the *Albuquerque Daily Citizen* was moved to quip that "if Grant Gillett . . . writes a book we presume that it will be bound in cowhide with the tail inside."[83]

This failure may have induced Elfego Baca to enter the case, which had received much publicity in New Mexico. Baca was no stranger to northern Mexico. He had both mining investments and friends in the region, among them Charles F. Hunt, a former Bernalillo County sheriff. Hunt had been forced to resign in 1895 when his bondsmen began to suspect him of financial irregularities and withdrew their support. He had settled in Mexico. Within days of the arrival of Grant Gillett in Chihuahua, Hunt made his acquaintance and soon engaged in a separate business venture with the notorious "Kansas cattle plunger." When Arnold and Troxel embarked upon their unsuccessful trip to Kansas City, Gillett's new partner went along. Elfego Baca sought out Charles F. Hunt at the latter's bar in Parral, in southern Chihuahua, and proposed that they earn the bounty on the fugitive speculator. This shadowy saloon man proposed to bring into the plot a budding rustler and bandit, Pancho Jaime (later known as Pancho Villa). No sooner had Elfego and Villa been introduced than the livestock thief had the audacity to try to sell him stolen mules. The two men eventually joined forces and devised a plan to kidnap Gillett, turn him over to the American authorities, and divide the spoils. The State of Kansas, however, revoked the reward before the two conspirators could carry out their plot, recalled Elfego.[84]

The bounty hunter's memory erred on several points, although there is no reason to doubt his interest in this case. Grant Gillett, who came from a prominent Kansas family, desperately desired to return to the United States, and a life of respectability. He invested in mining property in the Parral District, made a new fortune, and reopened negotiations with his creditors in the United States. On 1 February 1904, the *New York Times* reported that Gillett had invited a committee of his creditors to Mexico in order to inspect his new holdings. He gained more headlines in the following May when he was seen in the company of Doctor R. C. Flower, a New York physician and mining speculator, who had fled grand larceny charges. A whisper of murder also accompanied Flower, a known associate of Grant Gillett in other enterprises. However, the clever Gillett had stolen the Baca-Villa combination's thunder. In August 1904 (not 1906 as Baca recalled), Gillett turned over his Parral mines to his Kansas creditors. He still had a small fortune left over when he returned to the United States. Gillett died on a posh estate in Las Angeles County, California, in 1925.[85]

As an attorney, Baca enjoyed much more success and popularity. In the first decade of this century, his practice grew steadily and his reputation for success, especially in criminal cases, was very good. In January 1908, the *Daily New Mexican* of Santa Fe noted the arrival of Elfego and went on to remark that he "is rapidly forging to the front in the legal profession." When this promising man-at-the-bar arrived in Socorro in the following July to take a case, the local newspaper observed that Baca "will doubtless exercise his well known skill in criminal cases to the best possible advantage in defense of his client." The fees of Elfego's clients, this same editor remarked later, are "well invested." In a biographical sketch in a special issue of the *Albuquerque Morning Journal* in February 1912, one journalist noted Baca's "remarkable success" but added that he had continued to study the law "very hard, even after the time when such work is considered necessary."[86]

In 1898 he took the case of William "Bronco Bill" Walters, one of the Southwest's most infamous highwaymen. Walters was accused of the robbery of a train near Belen and the murder of three pursuing lawmen, one of whom was Francisco X. Vigil, a Valenica County deputy sheriff. Whether the outlaw requested Baca as his defense counsel is not known. The choice was an intriguing one, since this noted Hispano had won much fame in a shootout with Anglo cowhands in 1884, and he had continued to champion the native community against such interlopers. Perhaps Baca accepted this task as a means to antagonize the leaders of Valencia County—the Luna family—against whom he had harbored a grudge since (Baca believed) these powerful persons had persecuted his father in the early 1880s. As a professional man of the law, he may have allowed no personal feelings to enter into his decision. The Bronco Bill case was difficult. Train robbery was a capital offense in New Mexico, and the murder of Vigil, a member of a prominent Valencia County family, would almost certainly yield the sentence of death. Baca succeeded in obtaining a change of venue to Chaves County—a heavily Anglo area—where Walters pleaded "not guilty" to a charge of assault with a deadly weapon. His case was then removed to Socorro in November 1899, whereupon Elfego Baca relinquished the matter to Humphrey B. Hamilton, his former mentor. Walters pleaded guilty to murder in the second degree, and Judge Charles A. Leland sentenced him to life imprisonment.[87]

In the previous summer, Elfego Baca had accompanied the judge to Roswell for a session of court. Leland, a resident of Ohio, was new to the southwestern frontier and had some misgivings about western gunmen. He offered Baca ten dollars a day to serve as interpreter and bodyguard; Baca had planned to attend this session anyway. Years later, he informed a Works Projects Administration interviewer that Leland was so anxious about his safety that "he would hardly go to the corner store for a cigar or a newspaper without his interpreter." While in Roswell, Baca took the case of two Texas sheepmen who had signed the bond of a third party, a Hispano, who had fled the county. These nervous sureties offered him $500 to find some means to relieve them of this obligation. The crafty lawyer quietly substituted another man, a Mexican citizen, for the defendant. Judge Leland, to whom all persons of Spanish-American descent evidently looked alike, failed to detect this bit of skullduggery, fined the impostor, and let him go. Baca's clients, who were not a party to this piece of trickery and did not know this Mexican, were astounded at the latter's presence before the bar of justice. "You made a mistake," they said after the trial. "What the Hell do you care?" replied Baca, "The case is settled, isn't it?"[88]

Elfego Baca later claimed to have successfully defended nineteen men charged with murder. While this may have been an exaggeration, considerable time was required to prepare such cases. In December 1904, Baca wrote Secundino Romero, District Court clerk in Las Vegas, New Mexico, for information concerning Epimenio Garcia, recently killed in Socorro County. Baca was defending the man charged in Garcia's death and desired background information about the victim. Baca informed Romero that he had heard that Garcia had been "a member of that old gang that created much disturbance in your city some years ago," and the attorney wanted to know if any "indictments [were] pending against him in your Court." Baca also requested the names of "persons of good standing . . . who will testify to his [Garcia's] bad reputation."[89]

The experienced frontier lawyer realized that much more than the facts were required to win the freedom of a client in a murder trial. Writer Agnes Morley Cleaveland had firsthand experience with Elfego Baca's courtroom tactics. In her delightful volume, *No Life for a Lady*, Morely described his defense of her friend, Corky, who killed a man in Socorro County shortly after the turn of the century. The victim, named McCullough, had refused to pay a debt. Agnes, daughter of rancher Ray Morley, was subpoenaed as a witness. Baca, who "spoke halting English," instructed her carefully what to say on the witness stand. When she proposed merely to tell the truth, Baca replied in surprise, "'Nobody tell what he know in a *murder* trial." Instead, "*They* lie, *we* lie, *everybody* lie," he asserted. This interested woman was dismayed at the casualness of both prosecution and defense and feared the worst for her friend. Baca assured her that he placed three men on the jury—nine were Hispanos—who "won't give in—not eef the roof fall on them." True to his promise, the jury could not agree, and Corky was remanded to the custody of the sheriff for a new trial. While the defendant awaited his second appearance before the bench, Elfego Baca withdrew as Corky's defense attorney and suddenly appeared on the other side of the case, as the public prosecutor. In 1905 the governor appointed Baca as the district attorney. But Baca then dismissed Corky's case. To be free from the court did not mean freedom from the lawyers, who demanded their fees. They took his small ranch and all of his cattle. Corky died shortly thereafter in Magdalena. Cleaveland may have taken some literary liberties with this story when she alleged that Baca did not speak English clearly. His years in Topeka had trained him well in the language.[90]

Elfego Baca's political star continued to rise in the early years of the twentieth century. He was a power to be reckoned with in Socorro and influential in the territorial Republican Party. In August 1898, Joseph F. Towle, office deputy of Sheriff Holm O. Bursum, testified to this popularity in a report to his superior who was attending the Republican National Convention in Chicago. The political duet of Bursum and Elfego Baca apparently controlled a majority of the votes in Socorro County. Towle declared that everything was quiet. "It is claimed Elfego is in Mexico." The local newspapers had little to print, continued the deputy, since "you & Elfego were away & everyone did not know how to act. . . .You might as well enjoy yourself." When Governor Miguel A. Otero addressed the GOP nominating convention in 1900, Elfego Baca and an equally well known lawman, Patrick Floyd Garrett, received the joint honor of escorting the territorial executive into the convention hall.[91]

On 17 March 1905, Governor Miguel A. Otero appointed Elfego Baca to the prestigious office of district attorney for Socorro and Sierra counties. Aspiring politicians considered this post as an important stepping stone to higher office. Some political influence was necessary to reach this milestone, and Baca evidently obtained the nod of Holm O. Bursum, the Socorro County Republican boss. The memory of Baca's bid somehow found its way into the papers of a congressional committee which gathered evidence concerning New Mexico's bid for statehood. According to this report:

> Mr. Elfego Baca wanted to be district attorney of Socorro County. He fought the administration [in Santa Fe] until they capitulated, and his reward was the district attorneyship of both Socorro and Sierra counties—the salary of one office was not large enough to satisfy him.

Baca "is now boss of both counties," concluded the document. Many Anglos in Socorro County resented the influence of their district attorney. This prejudice was reflected in the writings of Eugene Manlove Rhodes, a cowhand and constitutent of District Attorney Baca. In his novelette, *Hit the Line Hard*, which appeared in 1915, Rhodes thinly disguised Elfego Baca in the character of Octaviano Baca, a crooked Socorro attorney. While the novelist admitted that he took "great liberties" in this characterization, Rhodes was serious about the portrayal of Socorro officials as very corrupt. "Elfego Baca ruled it [Socorro] in fiction," concluded W. H. Hutchinson, Rhodes's biographer, "as he did for many years in life."[92]

The new district attorney soon won a reputation as a crusader for timely issues in the turn-of-the-century Southwest. "Respectable" citizenry demanded the cleanup of "the sporting crowd," to include drinking and gambling establishments, prostitution, and gun carrying. In February 1906, the *Albuquerque Evening Citizen* noted that Baca was "After the 'Soiled-Doves' of Socorro." Baca "is making a vigorous and determined effort" to purge his town of "very undesirable characters," said this journalist, who urged "every officer of the law" to assist the ambitious attorney. In the following month, the same journal reported that Baca "is hot after pistol 'toters," and added that Baca had extended the no-gun order to lawmen "when not actually in the performance of duty." This stringent policy "meets the approval of all law-abiding citizens," insisted the *Citizen*.[93]

Whether peace officers should be free to carry weapons at all times or only when in actual performance of duties was a matter of some debate in New Mexico Territory. Baca took the extreme position. In March 1906, he ordered Socorro County Undersheriff Henry Dreyfuss to arrest Charles V. Mallet, a federal officer empowered to enforce the laws against Chinese aliens. The charges were "carrying and especially displaying a six-shooter" and resisting arrest. Enemies of the district attorney charged that he brought about this arrest out of personal spite. Mallet, not Baca, had been selected to make the opening remarks of welcome at a livestockmen's reception for the governor in Socorro. Indeed, Baca, a public official, was not even invited to this gathering.[94]

Such an attack upon his public name infuriated Elfego Baca, who sprang to his own defense in a letter to the *Albuquerque Evening Citizen*:

> The laws of the territory clearly and specifically define who are allowed to carry deadly weapons. I fail to see anything anywhere in the laws which makes a Chinese inspector immune. The self same culprit has been carrying a pistol during the entire period of time he has been in San Marcial. He has been seen with it on his person while singing in the church choir during holy services (no Chinese present to inspect). If the law should, in any way, and I claim it does not, allow Chinese inspectors to carry arms while on duty, there certainly is no excuse for carrying one in church.

Baca added that Mallet "carried his pistol to a dance which . . . the governor attended—no Chinese present." To add to Mallet's discomfort, the district attorney pointed out that C. E. Mead, who went on the defendant's bond (and was a member of the reception committee for the governor) was presently charged with selling liquor without a license in San Marcial. "The law is no respecter of persons," continued the angry barrister, and "I will do my duty, according to law, without malice, prejudice or jealousy."[95]

District Attorney Baca had set the wheels of justice in motion and due process had to be fulfilled. The Mallet case was continued to the fall 1906 term of district court. Even though Baca had resigned his position by this time, a Socorro jury persisted in convicting Charles Mallet and thus vindicating the former district attorney. The circle of federal officials was much dismayed at this slap. Assistant United States District Attorney E. L.

Medler, who had unsuccessfully defended Mallet, attempted to win the governor's intervention through the good offices of Mounted Police Captain Fred Fornoff. In a letter of 12 December, Medler recounted the accusation that Elfego Baca was guilty of a malicious prosecution and furthermore, that he was still "stirring up a lot of trouble" in Socorro. Far from being a gunman, Mallet was a "young, serious-minded [*sic*]" officer and authorized to carry weapons. Medler pointed out that this conviction resulted from an all-Hispano jury in Socorro. "In view of . . . Baca's well-known influence among the Mexicans here," wrote Medler, this decision "was not unexpected." This angry lawyer urged the police captain to ask Governor Herbert Hagerman to look into the matter. District Judge Frank W. Parker eventually dismissed Mallet's case in December 1907, at the plaintiff's expense.[96]

This much-publicized case merely highlighted the controversial nature of Elfego Baca's tenure in the district attorneyship. A Socorro dispatch of 12 April 1906 reported that Baca had just telegraphed his resignation to Governor Hagerman, effective 15 May. Hagerman, who had only recently assumed office, had begun a general house cleaning among appointive officials. "Mr. Baca had not been asked to resign," according to this reporter, "but it is understood that he anticipated such a request." He merely avoided the embarrassment of the inevitable. In his recollections, Baca volunteered few facts about this brief stint as public prosecutor, except to say that "it was difficult to serve as District Attorney." Elfego Baca's legal talents were immediately requested by the Sierra County Cattlemen's Association, which desired his services in the dangerous task of prosecuting rustlers.[97]

The repercussions from this crusading attorney's outspoken and abrasive behavior continued after he departed office. On 30 June 1906, an anonymous Socorran informed the *El Paso News* that word "has leaked out here that Hon. Elfego Baca, . . . has filed charges of a serious character against Sheriff Leandro Baca of Socorro county." While Baca was only the agent for a group of concerned citizens who brought charges against the sheriff, this report placed Elfego in the uncomfortable position of moving against a relative, apparently a cousin. In August the former district attorney presented to Governor Herbert J. Hagerman a long list of charges against Leandro Baca, including misfeasance and malfeasance in office. This lawman, who hailed from a locally prominent family and had presided over the sheriff's office since 1902, had also reportedly developed a drinking problem. After an investigation into these charges by Mounted Police Captain John Fullerton, the governor removed Leandro Baca on 6 October 1906 and appointed a replacement.[98]

There was apparently much more than the mere ouster of a sheriff in this case, and Elfego Baca was in the center of the turmoil. The movement to remove the chief county lawman had revealed the existence of two factions within the local Republican Party. On 7 July 1906, the *Albuquerque Evening Citizen* announced that "A Holy Political War" was under way in the county to the south and that Elfego Baca was one of the targets in this intraparty struggle. The Socorro County Board of Commissioners had just given Baca three days to move out of his office in the courthouse. Apparently he had continued to occupy this office space since his term as district attorney, but had paid no rent. To add to his embarrassment, the county commissioners instructed the sheriff, Leandro Baca, whom Elfego was presently trying to oust, "to enforce the order."[99]

In a written reply, the testy lawyer refused to comply until the new district attorney and the judge returned. Elfego declared that these officials had left him in charge when they were called away on judicial business. Furthermore, he added, the commissioners' order to vacate was not issued "in good faith." Instead, the county fathers used this means as a reprisal for Baca's charges against Sheriff Leandro Baca. The *Citizen* reporter remarked that Elfego "has gained quite a reputation throughout the territory by his open letters on subjects in which he is interested" and predicted a "lively" fight between the "ins" and "outs" in the next elections in Socorro County. Presumably, this matter was resolved in due course, but probably at Elfego Baca's pace.[100]

By this time, Elfego Baca had amassed an impressive record of public offices in Socorro County, and he and his family were a recognized part of Socorro's Hispano social circle. The two communities—Anglo and Spanish-American—seldom fraternized socially, if Socorro's society columns give an accurate reflection of the polite company that prominent persons kept. Nonetheless, the movements of Elfego and his family between Socorro and Albuquerque were regularly reported. In January 1906, one journalist noted that Baca's daughter, Josephine, had just received "a handsome present" from A. A. Freeman, her father's law partner. The gift was "an elegant filigree bracelet" worthy of a "princess." In the following month, Elfego Baca's wife was observed sponsoring a ball in honor of a guest from Albuquerque.[101]

By 1906 Elfego Baca had become an established fixture in the legal and political circles of New Mexico Territory. More than two decades had passed since he had sprung into prominence as a result of his standoff of the murderous cowboys at San Francisco Plaza. After a stint as a law enforcer, he had joined the ranks of the legal fraternity and set off on a very successful career at the bar. And if he still displayed some of the temperament of the rough-hewn southwestern frontiersmen, he nonetheless possessed the qualities necessary to hold any number of important public offices. His growing ambition or his quarrel with fellow Republicans in Socorro, or both, may have persuaded him to relocate to Albuquerque in summer 1906. No doubt tempers were hot in the politically volatile county, and Elfego may have concluded that a strategic withdrawal—reminiscient of his abrupt departure in 1885—was the discreet thing to do. A convenient pretext for the relocation of his family occurred in July 1906, at the very time of his quarrel with fellow Republicans. A series of severe earth tremors struck Socorro County, causing much alarm in the county seat. Elfego and his wife and children, as well as Assessor Abe Baca, took refuge in Albuquerque. On 17 July, the *Albuquerque Evening Citizen* noted their arrival and remarked that the Bacas were "very much alarmed over the frequency of the earthquake."[102]

CHAPTER FOUR

REVOLUTIONARY YEARS

If Elfego Baca considered Albuquerque a place where more opportunities were open to him, he was not disappointed. His fortunes continued to grow. He had always worked conscientiously for the betterment of the Spanish-American people. As early as 1892, he had invested in a Spanish-language newspaper in Albuquerque, *La Opinion Publica*. This journal remained one of the most successful of its type in the territory. Shortly after relocating to Albuquerque, he assumed the position of publisher and manager. In noting this change, the *Socorro Chieftain* remarked that "It goes without saying that Mr. Baca will give [a] good account of himself in his new capacity." In March 1910, he became sole owner of this press and brought a son-in-law, John B. McGuiness, into the business. In describing Elfego Baca's style as an editor, the *Albuquerque Evening Citizen* noted that he wrote "with ease and fluency" and with "a peculiar rhythm." He was "the equal of any" newspaper editor in New Mexico, concluded the writer. When Baca and his fellow Spanish-language editors formed a professional association in the following year, he was elected treasurer. In 1912, this organization joined with Anglo journalists to establish the precursor to the New Mexico Press Association.[103]

In December 1907 he joined others in the formation of New Mexico's first chapter of the *Alianza Hispania-Americana* (Spanish- American Alliance), an important sign of Hispanic solidarity.

The goal of the Alliance, which was headquartered in Tucson, Arizona, was the familiarization of the Hispanos with the American constitutional process—furthering the statehood movement. The organization desired to assist the Spanish-Americans "in a charitable way." Since Baca was residing in Albuquerque at the time, he became the director of the Bernalillo County branch. In September 1908 Baca represented the alliance at the National Irrigation Congress in Albuquerque, which helped to initiate a movement for flood control and other benefits for the Rio Grande Valley.[104]

While the prestige and popularity of Elfego Baca was growing in New Mexico, he retained the abrupt and confrontive personality of his youth. This characteristic surfaced in an altercation with C. E. Gleckler in May 1908. Some time after Baca had leased the second floor of Gleckler's office building on Fourth Street in Albuquerque for *La Opinion Publica*, the landlord had ordered him to vacate. Baca did so with the understanding that he had until 15 May to complete the process. One day prior to this date, several persons observed Gleckler "dash down stairs" and out into the street in front of Elfego's newly rented quarters. He informed a passerby that Elfego pulled a pistol on him "without provocation." This confrontation evidently arose over some misunderstanding about the keys to the old office and Gleckler's having thrown out some items that Baca had not yet retrieved. Baca and Gleckler had retired to the lawyer's new office to obtain the keys when this new crisis occurred.[105]

When a reporter for the *Albquerque Citizen* questioned Elfego about his former landlord's accusations, he replied:

> I noticed that he [Gleckler] kept his hand in his overcoat pocket and appeared to be angry. . . .I was satisfied that he had a pistol in his overcoat pocket, holding it with his hand. I went to the [new] office. . . .I asked him to be seated and he curtly refused. I got the keys and pretended to hand them to him. As I did so, I let them fall to the floor. Mr. Gleckler stooped to pick them up. I grasped him by the wrist, jerked his hand from his overcoat pocket and wrenched the pistol from his grasp. He had been holding it concealed in his overcoat pocket.

As a man inexperienced in the ways of gunmen and lawmen, Gleckler had made a very indiscreet move—he kept his hands in his coat. He informed the journalist that he kept them there "because they were cold." He had no weapon, the angry property owner added, and did not own one. "I cannot account for Mr. Baca acting as he did," concluded Gleckler. The *Citizen* reporter had some fun at his expense. "If anybody expects to get the start on Attorney Elfego Baca in a gun play," said the journalist, "he will find it necessary to get up early. . . .The question now is, who owns the gun?" Gleckler decided not to press charges, believing (erroneously) that Elfego would eventually "repent of his hasty actions."[106]

This aggressive man continued to be newsworthy and kept the Albuquerque citizenry entertained. A few months later, he was involved in an accident. A city fire-fighting wagon ran into his buggy, upset the rig, and broke two of Elfego's ribs. He later admitted that this accident "bunged him up badly" and "should by all rights have finished him," but a local newspaper reported him back on a regular work schedule within only two months. In the following March 1909, the injured man filed a $5,000 law suit against the City of Albuquerque. The outcome of this legal action is not known.[107]

Politics remained Elfego Baca's passion, and he sought opportunities to wield influence constantly. In December 1907, he attended the convention that would eventually lead to statehood for New Mexico. George Curry, former sheriff and now territorial governor, presided at the convention. In a repeat of past convention practices, Elfego was chosen as one of the delegates to escort the newly selected officers to their positions. No doubt Baca was disappointed when Governor Curry neglected to choose him as one of the more than one hundred persons to travel to the national capital and press for immediate admission.[108]

When the United States Congress authorized New Mexico to begin preparations for statehood in June 1910, ambitious politicians began a scramble for the new offices that resulted from this coveted status. In view of the territory's meager population of 200,000, New Mexico would receive only two seats in the House of Representatives, along with the usual two senatorial chairs. Elfego Baca sought the Republican nomination for one of the congressional positions. He faced considerable competition from former Governor George Curry and a Deming newspaperman, Ralph C. Ely. Furthermore, several bosses of the territorial Republican Party did not approve of Baca, presumably because of his Hispanic origins. These politicos, however, felt compelled to go through the motions of recognizing the important Spanish-American population. At the Republican nominating convention in Las Vegas, in September 1911, Albert B. Fall, a leading GOP political light (and former Democrat), formally nominated Baca. In his speech, Fall paid "eloquent tribute to the Spanish-Americans of New Mexico," recalled George Curry. But Curry believed that this gesture was merely ritualistic, and that the Republican leaders favored Curry and Ely and intended to select them all along. A complication arose when a rift appeared in the party ranks. Thomas Benton Catron, one of the most influential men in New Mexico, disliked not only Curry but Elfego Baca as well. The votes that Catron and his followers diverted from the majority bloc apparently upset the plans of the bosses. In the final canvassing of all Republicans in the territory, Curry and Baca won the nod as the nominees in the race for the House of Representatives. The Democratic Party (joined by some maverick Republicans) nominated Harvey B. Fergusson, an Albuquerque lawyer and former territorial delegate, and Paz Valverde, an influential Hispano.[109]

The electioneering began in earnest in early October 1911. George Curry recalled that the competition was "bitter," while historian Benjamin M. Read, a contemporary of these events, candidly admitted that "in the history of disreputable political contests in the United States its equal cannot be named." The candidates resorted to "slander, vilification and personalities." As a Republican, Elfego Baca was hindered by several unfortunate circumstances. Former Governor Herbert J. Hagerman and his small following had bolted the Republican Party and joined the Democrats. Furthermore, the so-called "Blue Ballot" had become a sticky issue. This controversial resolution of Congress provided the New Mexico voters with the ability to amend the new state constitution with relative ease. It came in response to complaints that powerful corporate interests in the state constitutional convention had influenced the delegates to make amendments virtually impossible. Presumably, these unnamed groups desired to reduce the allegedly ignorant Spanish-speaking community from exercising any future influence through changes to the new state constitution. Unfortunately, Elfego Baca may have failed to comprehend the full import of the Blue Ballot to many New Mexico voters. George Curry recalled that Baca followed the lead of the GOP's condemnation of the controversial resolution in his acceptance speech at the nominating convention, whereas Curry merely trimmed his sails on the issue. Although most Republican candidates for new state positions were defeated, George Curry managed to win his congressional seat with 30,162 votes. Harvey Fergusson, the Democrat, won the second seat with 29,999 votes, while Baca polled 28,836 and Paz Valverde, 28,353.[110]

The defeat obviously stung Elfego Baca, and he could hardly be expected to shake off this setback. This play for the House of Representatives was his first bid for high office. Through the columns of his newspaper, *La Opinion Publica*, he struck out at the Republican Party, which he accused of a "double cross," and especially George Curry, whom Baca asserted "did not exactly tote fair in the recent campaign."

> Curry's work in the last campaign was marvelous [Baca editorialized]. He was a democrat among the democrats; he was a republican among the republicans, and he was a progressive among the progressives. In the so-called American towns in Eddy, Chaves, Roosevelt and Curry counties he even sought to raise the race issue, saying it would be well to vote for him and Fergusson [the Democrat] in order to prevent a native New Mexican from going to Congress.

As a consequence of this chameleon-like posture, added Baca, Curry would be in an enviable position in Congress. "No party will have the right to claim him," concluded the defeated candidate. Curry "will serve there as the joker in a poker game." The *Albuquerque Evening Journal*, which reprinted Elfego's article, admitted that Baca was "slightly angry" but concluded in a somewhat scolding tone that he was being "peevish" about this matter.[111]

Elfego Baca continued to faithfully serve the Republican cause, although not without controversy. In March 1912, a bizarre incident took place in Santa Fe, when the Central Committee of the territorial Republican Party announced that it had uncovered evidence implicating four state representatives, two from Taos and two from Rio Arriba counties, in a bribery scheme. According to first reports, these four legislators saw a chance to make money in the approaching elections for the first two United States senators from New Mexico. The selection would take place in the state assembly—this election preceded the amendment that provided for direct election—and there were many candidates, among them Albert B. Fall. This foursome reportedly demanded $1,250 each in return for their votes for Fall. As the facts of this case became known, Elfego Baca's name became very prominent in the exposure of this alleged plot. Not only did he make the accusations, but it transpired that Baca served as the emissary between the conspiratorial quartet and the Republican Party leaders who allegedly desired to ensnare the crooked politicos. When the news broke on 23 March 1912, the *Socorro Chieftain* averred that "Much credit belongs to Judge Albert B. Fall and Attorney Elfego Baca."[112]

The arrest and jailing of the four assemblymen not only came as a shock to many citizens but created a furor among their friends and supporters. The trial was held in the New Mexico House of Representatives, from 20 to 29 March 1912, under very strained circumstances. Benjamin M. Read, the historian, was one of the attorneys for the defense. Read was notably contemptuous of Elfego Baca's part in the entrapment and referred to him as "one Elfego Baca," as though he were a low-level and unknown party hack. Some observers soon concluded that the entire incident was merely a seamy political ploy. As one newspaper remarked, the purpose of this plot was to unseat the four representatives and thus prevent them from "voting for their preference for United States senators"; that is, to deprive them of the opportunity to vote against Albert B. Fall. This writer was especially critical of the witnesses, which presumably included Elfego Baca, who failed to present "clear and concise" testimony.

The reinstatement of the accused solons was greeted with "unalloyed satisfaction," declared one journalist. Albert B. Fall and Thomas B. Catron were elected United States senators. While Elfego later claimed that he was "given credit in some quarters for electing Fall," there is little doubt that this unsavory affair did some harm to his reputation in the new state. Baca could take some consolation in the fact that he was admitted to practice in the United States Supreme Court about this time.[113]

Elfego Baca was not above using his official influence on behalf of relatives. Nepotism knew no bounds in the fierce politics of the southwestern territories. Politicians assumed that family members were the most trustworthy appointees to public office. Elfego Baca had many relatives in official positions. One brother, Abdenago, served fifteen years as tax assessor of Socorro County. Two of Elfego's cousins, Cipriano and Leandro Baca (brothers), became lawmen. Cipriano served as a deputy United States marshal, deputy sheriff, and as the first sheriff of Luna County in 1899. When the Mounted Police were organized in 1905, he received an appointment as a lieutenant in this first territory-wide law enforcement body. Mary Foraker, daughter of Creighton Foraker, the last United States marshal of New Mexico Territory, recalled how she and her friends watched with "eyes agog" when the famous Cipriano visited her father in Albuquerque.[114]

Leandro, brother of Cipriano, suffered some setbacks in his law enforcement career, as his removal from the Socorro County shrievalty revealed. Leandro, however, soon obtained a place in the Mounted Police and his career seemed back on track. Then the legislature suddenly announced that budget reductions were necessary and the number of policemen would have to be reduced. Leandro Baca lost his post. In December 1909, Elfego Baca appealed to Fred Fornoff, the Mounted Police captain, and asked that he use his good offices to try to persuade Governor George Curry to reinstate Leandro. Elfego Baca admitted that he had opposed Leandro Baca politically—the writer said nothing about being related—but assured Fornoff that the former sheriff had promised never to drink again. "Mr. [Leandro] Baca is a poor man; [but] a very honorable man," affirmed Elfego Baca. His plea evidently fell upon deaf ears, and Leandro Baca returned to Socorro County as a deputy sheriff.[115]

Elfego Baca was a many-sided person and engaged in various pursuits besides of law and politics. He participated in many economic activities. Thomas B. Catron, who owned extensive properties in Socorro County, employed Baca to look after leases and other business matters. Baca sometimes listed his occupation as "mining promoter." In September 1891, the *Socorro Chieftain* reported that he and other investors had just made a silver strike near the mining camp of Kelly. They named the discovery the National Mine. He made other investments near Magdalena and Mogollon. He soon earned a reputation for his ability to assess the potential value of mines, and many companies enjoyed his services. He represented various American firms that hoped to capitalize upon discoveries in northern Mexico shortly after the turn of the century. On a trip to Parral, in Chihuahua, Baca took a nasty fall down a shaft that left him alone and unconscious for several hours. This experience terrified him. He confessed to his biographer that "none of his shooting scrapes" left him so shaken. Baca also invested in real estate in Socorro and Albuquerque and was involved in the construction of well-publicized office buildings in both cities after the turn of the century. In 1914 the City Directory of Albuquerque recorded him in one of his new facilities at 523 West Gold Avenue.[116]

In spite of his proclivity toward controversy, Elfego Baca continued to wield great influence in the Hispanic community of New Mexico. His reputation as a hard man ensured that he would take cases that might expose him to danger, while his reputation for winning difficult court cases served as an additional incentive to the prospective client. In February 1912, a street brawl took place in San Rafael, in Valencia County, when Constable Juan Chaves y Jaramillo attempted to arrest Manuel Padilla and his son, Zacarias. The two men withdrew to the family residence, whereupon the constable summoned a posse and lay siege to the Padilla home. Zacarias Padilla, who was a member of the state legislature, sent an urgent request for aid to Elfego Baca. When Baca arrived, he found the local lawman with sixteen armed possemen surrounding the house, while the Padillas were vowing to fight to the death. The lawyer "succeeded in his role as peacemaker," said an Albuquerque news report, and "effected a truce." In the process, Baca acquired the Padillas as clients, while Constable Jaramillo was charged with arbitrary arrest.[117]

Although he was a politician and lawyer for many years, Elfego Baca continued to provide law enforcement services. Some duties were very grim and not for the squeamish. On 16 May 1913, Bernalillo County Sheriff Perfecto Armijo faced the unhappy chore of hanging Demecio Delgadillo for murder. Armijo, who did not relish such a task, asked Elfego Baca to assist with the arrangements. William A. Keleher, who covered the execution for an Albuquerque newspaper, met Baca formally for the first time at this grisly site. Keleher described the veteran lawman-lawyer's title as that of *bastonero*, which in English means "master of ceremonies." Baca supervised "all arrangements down to the most minute detail," said Keleher, to include building the scaffold, testing the noose rope, and standing by during the actual event. After the attending physician pronounced the victim dead, Baca announced to the onlookers, "Gentlemen, the official time is three minutes and sixteen seconds. . . .Gentlemen, this is one of the nicest hangings I have ever seen. Everything went off beautifully." Baca was not permitted to enjoy this moment of public attention, however. The attending priest, apparently concerned about the effects of this terrible duty upon Baca's soul, rose to inquire about his spiritual health. The *bastonero* was obviously chagrined at such attention, "made his way through the . . . spectators," and quickly walked away.[118]

In addition to his many affairs in New Mexico, Elfego Baca had maintained business connections in Mexico for many years. As early as 1902, his official letterhead listed a branch law office in the border community of El Paso. The outbreak of the Mexican Revolution in 1911 aroused his interest as well as his emotions, and Elfego soon demonstrated a strong partisanship for the cause of Francisco Madero and Pascual Orozco. At the ouset of the disturbances at Ciudad Juarez, just across the international boundary from El Paso, Elfego again met Pancho Villa. The outlaw leader joined the Madero movement at that place, but soon fell out with the *junta*. Relations between Baca and Villa also cooled when Baca failed to keep an appointment with the rebel. Villa wanted Elfego to guard some valuables—possibly money and jewels—for him until the disturbance in Mexico ended. In a fit of pique the revolutionary then placed a $30,000 bounty on his former friend, according to Elfego. If Baca can be believed, he countered this insult by arranging the theft of one of the Mexican's prized rifles.[119]

In a further move calculated to arouse Villa's anger, Baca accepted a retainer from his new political rival, Victoriano Huerta. This new association brought almost immediate work and financial dividends. In January 1914, United States authorities arrested General Jose Ynez Salazar, a Huerta follower, in Sanderson, Texas. Salazar was charged with violation of the American neutrality laws and placed in a detention center at Fort Bliss, near El Paso. When Elfego Baca arrived at Fort Bliss to consult with his client, General Hugh Scott, who commanded United States forces along the border, refused him entry. Only a telegram from New Mexico Senator Albert B. Fall persuaded the stubborn general to relent.[120]

In the meantime, news of Baca's close relations with the Mexican revolutionaries had reached the United States Congress. The House Committee on Foreign Affairs summoned him to testify in regard to the confused conditions along the border. On 15 March, the *New York Times* reported that Baca had answered questions on the previous day. In regard to Pancho Villa, the New Mexican declared that he "was a bandit and always would be." In reference to the outlaw's penchant for appropriating livestock, Baca sparked a laugh from the committee members when he quipped that Villa "sold cattle, but never bought any." In regard to the existence of distrust between Villa and Venustiano Carranza, the witness declared that the latter "was so afraid of Villa that he would not sleep with him [Villa]." Baca averred that Huerta was the only leader who could preside over Mexico, not because he was the best man but the strongest figure.[121]

General Salazar's case lingered in the United States Court for several months. In November 1914, the army transferred him to a detention camp at Fort Wingate, New Mexico. Later that month, the United States marshal delivered him to the Bernalillo County Jail in Albuquerque to answer charges of perjury. On 20 November friends of the rebel general assisted him in a widely publicized jailbreak. Two masked men surprised Deputy Sheriff Charles Armijo and handcuffed him to a post. A second deputy had been lured away a few minutes earlier by a mysterious telephone call. General Salazar then rode away in a buggy, while his accomplices attempted to mislead pursuit by taking a taxicab to another part of the city. The escapee went into hiding on the ranch of Celestino Otero, a Salazar supporter, near Albuquerque. Salazar eventually made his way to Mexico where he issued a *pronunciamiento* for a new revolution.[122]

The successful flight of General Salazar embarrassed the administration of President Woodrow Wilson. Within a few days, Department of Justice investigators were on the scene in Albuquerque. The finger of suspicion pointed to many persons, some of whom were locally prominent. Federal authorities charged Elfego Baca and five other men with conspiracy to free General Salazar, who was a prisoner of the United States marshal at the time. Among the indictees were the district attorney, state game warden, and others. Elfego later declared that a mysterious female, Senorita Margarita, was also involved in the plot, but she apparently successfully eluded the police. The Spanish-American community of New Mexico sprang to the defense of Elfego Baca and his fellow indictees. The defendants employed Octaviano A. Larrazolo, a leading Hispanic politician and former Mexican citizen, to prepare their defense. Baca maintained that he was patronizing a local saloon at the time of the breakout. He explained the escape by saying that Salazar's followers in Mexico had become frustrated at Baca's inability to obtain the release of his client on a writ of habeas corpus. These Salazar partisans secretly entered New Mexico and had spirited their leader away. Baca and his comrades were tried in Santa Fe in December 1915. An all-Hispano jury quickly exonerated them. The efforts of Elfego Baca to protect General Salazar under the American laws went for nought. The Mexican patriot died rather ignominiously a short time later.[123]

The liberation of General Salazar and the association of Elfego Baca and other prominent New Mexicans with the case had some locally significant consequences. According to historian Ralph H. Vigil, who studied the Salazar case, Manuel U. Vigil, a codefendant with Elfego Baca, was a prominent district attorney and perhaps the most promising Hispano political leader in New Mexico. Even though he was acquitted, the adverse publicity associated with the trial destroyed his hopes for future high office. In an ironic twist, the trial promoted Elfego Baca's popularity. As "the principal figure in the conspiracy," says Ralph Vigil, the already legendary Baca continued to thrive on such controversies.[124]

In order to receive his fee for services to Salazar, Baca was constrained to travel to Washington, D. C., where, under rather unusual circumstances, he obtained the money from a vice president of the Riggs National Bank. When asked what he thought the amount should be, Baca replied, after a few studied moments, $30,000. The banker quickly filled out a deposit slip, and then admitted that this figure was very reasonable. He had been authorized to pay up to $100,000. William Keleher, lawyer friend of Baca, recalled that the latter "could only manage a sickly smile as he fumbled his way out of the bank." To add to his discomfiture, the United States district attorney in New Mexico initiated proceedings to disbar Baca from practice in federal courts. This effort failed.[125]

In the midst of these legal proceedings in New Mexico, Elfego Baca traveled to El Paso on family and business matters. While there, he became involved in a lethal encounter with Celestino Otero, a Salazar partisan. Baca shot Otero to death on Sunday, 31 January 1915, just a few weeks after General Salazar's escape from the Albuquerque jail. The facts of this tragic rencontre may never be fully uncovered, since Otero did not live long enough to give a statement. He died on the operating table. Elfego surrendered to the city police immediately and gave the newspapers a full account. Celestino Otero, whom Baca said he knew "slightly" in Albuquerque, approached the lawyer in the Paso del Norte Hotel on Sunday afternoon and asked to speak to Elfego privately. Baca later said that he detected a furtive or nervous countenance about Otero. When Baca introduced Otero to a friend, Dr. F. B. Romero, Otero further aroused Elfego's suspicions when he kept "his right hand in his overcoat pocket and hesitated to shake hands." Otero suggested that they retire to the saloon of M. Andujo, another Salazar supporter and a former Baca client. Baca agreed, concluding that the matter to be discussed must be Andujo's fee, which remained outstanding. Romero agreed to drive them. While Baca rode in the automobile, Otero insisted upon walking the short distance to Andujo's.[126]

As the vehicle pulled away from the hotel, Elfego saw a second man join Celestino Otero. Baca thought he recognized him as Silvestre Quevedo, another revolutionary who had spent some time in the Fort Bliss internment camp with Jose Ynez Salazar. Baca continued:

> Arriving in the vicinity of Andujo's place, we were detained by an engine crossing the street on the Santa Fe tracks. As we were about to move on, Otero and his companion hailed us from the sidewalk. We turned the machine around and drew close to the sidewalk. As we did so, Otero stepped forward and in Spanish made a vile remark about my mother. Saying this he drew back and from his pocket drew a pistol and fired. The ball passed through my coat on the left side.

Elfego Baca, a man very experienced in such situations, did not hesitate:

> Realizing that an attempt had been made on my life, I pulled my pistol and shot twice. Otero fell backwards. After my second shot the man lying on the sidewalk, asked me not to shoot again, and I returned my pistol to my pocket. Otero was about 10 feet from me at the time."[127]

In Baca's rendition of this event to Kyle Crichton some dozen years later, the gunman amended this original account. He added that he and Romero actually visited Andujo's bar, only to find the owner absent. This aroused the pair's suspicions, and Baca said, "Let's get out of here." Only then did the train block the automobile, at which time Otero "and several companions" appeared. Angry and cautious by this time, Baca said to Otero, "I'm damned tired of all this fooling around. What do you want with me? Come on! What do you want?" At this point, Baca stepped down from the automobile on the side opposite his assailant and walked around the rear of the vehicle. As he did so,

Otero opened fire, his single bullet grazing Baca's abdomen. "It was the last shot from Otero," concluded Baca, as his "two rapid bullets struck the heart of Otero." The shootist then sped to the home of his attorney and called the El Paso authorities.[128]

Baca's case received considerable regional coverage. The *El Paso Herald*, which noted his prior residency in the Pass City, described him as "one of the most prominent men in New Mexico and [who] came into special prominence as the attorney for Gen. Salazar." The New Orleans *Times-Picayune* erroneously reported Baca as a former speaker of the house in the New Mexico Assembly. Various stories circulated to explain this tragic killing. A connection with General Salazar's escape from the Albuquerque jail appeared logical. One rumor alleged that Otero had permitted Salazar to hide on his ranch near Albuquerque, but only for a price. When Otero became greedy and demanded more money, the *junta* ordered Elfego Baca to shut him up. Another story held that Baca and his coconspirators in the liberation of General Salazar became alarmed when the federal grand jury failed to indict Celestino Otero. They suspected that he had struck a deal with the federal prosecutor and decided that Elfego should eliminate him. A Santa Fe journal concluded contrarywise that Otero's attempt upon Baca's life "was the outcome of the determination of the [Pancho] Villa faction to 'get' Baca for his friendship with General Jose Ynez Salazar."[129]

Baca's attorneys attempted to deflect all revolutionary associations and charged that a clique of anonymous wealthy New Mexicans whom the defendant had offended in his newspaper, *La Opinion Publica*, employed Otero to kill him. Baca later resurrected the story of the Valencia County clan that (he believed) attempted to send his father to jail in 1881 as an explanation for the attempt on Elfego's life. While Baca averred that he hardly knew Celestino Otero, the latter's wife testified later—at Elfego's conspiracy trial in Santa Fe—that they were well acquainted in Albuquerque and that Baca owed her husband money. She implied that the reason her spouse confronted Baca was to collect this debt. The fact that Celestino Otero, who claimed to be a physician, had been earlier prosecuted in New Mexico for practicing without a license, not to mention that he had traveled under the alias of Pedro Abeytia, worked in Elfego Baca's favor.

On 25 January 1916, an El Paso jury concluded that he had fired in self-defense and found him not guilty.[130]

In spite of the formal exoneration of Elfego Baca in the Salazar and Otero cases, clearly the New Mexico lawyer was more deeply involved in the Mexican revolutionary movement than met the eye. His Hispanic background and sympathy for the less fortunate naturally inclined him to the side of the underclass in the southern republic. Recent research reveals that Baca was privy to plans to liberate General Salazar as early as June 1914, some five months before the jail delivery in Albuquerque. Baca later made light of the fact that he had cleverly hidden his participation in the plot by making his presence known at an Albuquerque saloon at the very time of the breakout. J. R. Galusha, then a city policeman, recalled later how Baca asked him for the time at this critical moment. During the search for General Salazar after the jailbreak, Baca deliberately attempted to mislead pursuing authorities by asserting that the general's revolutionary opponents had murdered him.[131]

CHAPTER FIVE

A TURN AT THE POLITICAL PUMP

In spite of Elfego Baca's prominence in political circles of New Mexico, he had never held the office of sheriff. He sought this powerful position in Bernalillo County in November 1916. He lost. The association of his name with the Salazar case and the shooting of Celestino Otero may have discouraged some voters. The sheriff's position carried many responsibilities, including the service of warrants, subpoenas, and other court process, the care and custody of prisoners, and the keeping of the peace. In addition, the sheriff served as "handyman" and performed any task that the board of supervisors demanded. As George Curry, a former sheriff recalled, the voters of New Mexico considered the shrievalty the most important office in the county.[132]

Following his defeat in Bernalillo County in 1916, Elfego Baca relocated again to Socorro and reentered the hurly-burly of local politics. In November 1918 he won election to the coveted sheriff's post. Baca later confessed that he was unsure about the reasons for this victory, but speculated that the electorate may have concluded that "it was his turn at the political pump." This victory must have meant a great deal to him, since Baca had first won acclaim as a Socorro County deputy sheriff in 1884.[133]

Many misconceptions exist about Elfego Baca's term as Socorro County sheriff. These erroneous notions arise from the fact that his highly colored recollections have provided the only account of this two-year term. Baca boasted that "He enforced the law in every way possible," to include the novel means "of arresting people who were indicted by letter." Baca declared that he ordered fugitives

> to come on [in] . . . before a certain day, and if they did not come he knew that they were going to resist an arrest and as it was his duty to enforce the law he went after them. And he also adopted a rule that any person charged with . . . any violation of the law . . . would be arrested [and brought] before a court . . . before or within 48 hours.

While Elfego professed to believe that the summons of wanted persons by mail was unusual in law enforcement circles, such a procedure was not uncommon. Sheriffs naturally preferred the voluntary surrender of wanted persons and often sent them verbal or written requests to appear at the next session of court. Not only did such a cooperative attitude save the time of the sheriff's staff, but the courts were sometimes more inclined to impose lighter sentences. Baca's boast about arrests within forty-eight hours may have been an electioneering gimmick, but could not have been taken seriously by the sheriff's constitutents.[134]

A series of brutal murders had been committed near Quemado, in western Socorro County, just a few days before Elfego Baca entered office. On 11 December 1918, Mrs. Clara Coleman, wife of rancher Henry Coleman, was found brutally shot to death. Don Oliver, described in one source as an Hispanic hired hand, was also found dead in the same room. This double murder caused a sensation in the western precincts. Henry Coleman, who was apparently estranged from his wife and often worked a good distance away from the ranch house for days at a time, was away from home at the time. Suspicion for these bloody deeds fell upon various persons in the neighborhood. Ben Oliver, a brother of one of the victims, filed several complaints before a local justice of the peace. Among the suspects was Frank Bourbonnaise, a French-Canadian and former Canadian Mounted policeman, who had reportedly quarreled with the Colemans over a fence. Other complaints were filed against two brothers, Oscar and Fred Caudill. Some believed that Henry Coleman had killed his wife and Oliver, suspecting them of being lovers in his absence. When it was demonstrated that Coleman had been in Magdalena on the eleventh and could not have committed the murders, others alleged that Coleman had hired his ranching partner, Sam Foster, to do his dirty work.[135]

Since these grisly killings took place some one hundred miles west of Socorro, the precinct authorities took the first formal action. A constable's posse made the first arrests. As was often the case of these local forces, the posse included friends and relatives of the diseased. Oscar Caudill recalled that Ben Oliver, brother of Don, and Sam Foster were among his arresting party. "They acted so strangely," wrote Caudill, "that I was alarmed." He feared that they intended to kill him. Upon arriving in Quemado, Caudill learned the reason. Frank Bourbonnaise had been shot and killed while in the custody of this same posse. Although the details of Bourbonnaise's death were not yet clear, rumor had it that Henry Coleman had committed this latest murder. The officers now feared that he would also try to assassinate the Caudills. Indeed, they came upon Coleman on the road to Quemado in a severe snowstorm, but managed to avoid the gunman. In Quemado Justice of the Peace Profanio Baca held a hearing which failed to find any evidence against the brothers, but Baca decided to place Oscar under bond anyway, since Coleman threatened that he would have Caudill rearrested. In early January 1919, a correspondent in Magdalena informed an Albuquerque newspaper that Oscar Caudill had been placed under a $5,000 bond and that Henry Coleman was "under a $10,000 bond for his appearance before the grand jury" in Socorro for the Bourbonnaise shooting.[136]

Henry Coleman possessed the reputation of a hard man, and Elfego Baca recalled that he was "one of the very last bad men of New Mexico." Coleman's real name was Henry Street Hudspeth. He was the half brother of Claude Benton Hudspeth, a cattleman and lawyer of El Paso, and newly elected United States congressman in 1918. His name had been given to a Texas county in 1917. Street Hudspeth had reportedly gotten into trouble and fled to New Mexico under the assumed name of Henry Coleman. While in the employ of cattle baron Israel King in Chihuahua, in April 1896, Mexican customs officials arrested Coleman along with his boss and another cowhand, John Reed. The three men were permitted to languish in an unhealthy Ciudad Juarez jail for months. King died shortly after bribing his way out, while Coleman gained his freedom only after another King employee, John Cox, engineered a successful jailbreak. The Mexican government eventually released Reed in September 1897. In the meantime, Coleman ranched near Deming, New Mexico, although neighboring cattlemen suspected that his herd was enlarged at their expense. In about 1910 Coleman became manager of the Half-Circle N Ranch in Socorro County. He and his wife (or companion), Clara, also owned ranch lands on Largo Creek, northwest of Quemado. Among his neighbors there was his old friend, John Cox. Stock raisers soon suspected Coleman of rustling, and Arthur T. Hannett, a young Gallup lawyer—and later governor of New Mexico—acquired the unenviable task of seeing that a writ of attachment was served upon the badman's livestock. As the story goes, Hannett could find no officer in the Socorro County Sheriff's Office willing to serve the papers. Hannett returned to Gallup empty-handed. Yet, for every person who might accuse Henry Coleman of criminal activities, another would testify to his generosity and good nature.[137]

Since Henry Coleman and the Caudills were under bond to appear before the district court in Socorro at the spring 1919 term, Sheriff Elfego Baca had the duty to see that warrants of arrest were served and that the suspects were delivered to the county seat. Leandro Baca, the former sheriff and now Elfego's deputy, fetched the Caudills from Magdalena in an automobile. Oscar Caudill recalled vividly the trip to Socorro. Deputy Baca feared an ambush and insisted that Oscar and Fred carry weapons in the car. "If you are molested on this trip," quipped Leandro Baca, "I aim to get in the first shot." However, no effort was made against this official party, which eventually reached the county seat. Leandro Baca arranged bonds for the brothers, who returned home. When no witnesses appeared against the Caudills in the spring term, the presiding judge continued the case until the next session. This decision placed Oscar Caudill and his brother in an uneasy situation, since Henry Coleman had also been released. Oscar Caudill approached Sheriff Elfego Baca, who "advised me to get a good gun for Hazel [his wife] and to carry one myself." Baca cautioned Caudill "not to let anybody else get the first shot" in a gunfight if Henry Coleman made a threatening move.[138]

The fact that Sheriff Elfego Baca had the duty of delivering Henry Coleman to the district court placed the lawman in a conspicuous light. Trouble might arise. The wanted man caused no problem, though, and Baca later boasted that Coleman "did come in and give up" on the lawman's written request. Presumably, the badman would have done the same for any sheriff, since he was still regarded as a law-abiding citizen. George Curry, a former sheriff and political adversary of Elfego Baca, recalled that the lawman's lenient treatment of the suspected murderer provoked some public indignation. Curry, who ran the Chambon Hotel in Socorro, remembered that the sheriff registered Coleman at his (Curry's) establishment rather than placing him in jail as required by law. The district judge refused to release Coleman on bail during his trial. Baca asked "that I take charge of him," said Curry. Curry implied that Sheriff Baca was bowing to outside pressure, perhaps the influential Hudspeths of Texas. The lawman "was friendly to Coleman," said George Curry accusingly. On one occasion the hotel keeper found himself in a very awkward position. Coleman reclaimed his pistol from Curry's desk, went on a drunken spree, and threatened to kill Prosecuting Attorney Harry Owen. The hotel man managed to disarm Coleman and put him to bed, but then insisted that Baca place the suspect in jail. That was "where he belonged," said Curry.[139]

While Curry's suspicions may be true, it was also a fact that Sheriff Baca took some steps to gather evidence against Coleman for his upcoming trial. The trials of those accused in the three killings created a sensation in Socorro County. When Henry Coleman's trial for the murder of Frank Bourbonnaise took place in spring 1919, his wealthy Texas relatives put in a personal appearance and provided financial assistance. Sam Foster testified on his partner's behalf and convinced the jury that the prisoner had made a move for a posseman's weapon and forced Coleman to fire in self-defense. The fact that the arresting officers had unwisely stopped with their prisoner at the Coleman residence—and thus placed Bourbonnaise within the grasp of Henry Coleman—apparently failed to move the jury. The gunman went free.

In January 1921, Oscar Caudill was again brought to court for the murder of Clara Coleman. No witnesses appeared and the judge instructed the jury to return a not guilty verdict. The financial demands of lawyers and prolonged absence from their ranch cost the Caudills dearly. Much of their livestock had wandered away or had been stolen.[140]

Elfego Baca's conduct in the Henry Coleman case may have harmed his political standing in Socorro County. In earlier frontier days, the county sheriffs had considerable latitude in the performance of their duties. Elfego continued to function in this manner, although the county commissioners and the public expected more responsible conduct. Former Sheriff George Curry, whose dislike of Baca cannot be ignored, believed that the lawman "let his friendship for Coleman lead him into a clear evasion of official duty." Had Coleman managed to do harm to District Attorney Owen after escaping from Curry's hotel, the public outcry against the careless sheriff would have been even greater. "I joined in this criticism," admitted Curry. He volunteered that "there was never any question of Baca's personal courage," but such a quality could not substitute for discretion in office.[141]

Trouble continued to pursue Henry Coleman. Residents of Socorro County could never rest assured that he was not somehow involved in the death of his wife and Don Oliver. He went to some lengths to become administrator of her property, since Clara Coleman had had title to her own land and cattle. Such problems did not affect Elfego Baca, who left any future difficulties with Henry Coleman to his successor, V. V. Tafoya, who assumed office on 1 January 1921. In the following March, Coleman was indicted under his real name, Street Hudspeth, for the theft of twelve head of cattle from H. H. Lyle. George W. Henderson, a ranching acquaintance of Coleman, was also indicted. While Henderson was acquitted, powerful forces were mustered against Coleman. The New Mexico Cattle Growers' Association and the Texas & Southwestern Cattle Association assisted in the prosecution and "the case was hotly contested," according to the *Socorro Chieftain*. The accused gunman promptly jumped his bond and, added the journalist, "is now a fugitive."[142]

Sheriff V. V. Tafoya had the unenviable task of running down outlaw Henry Coleman. Rather than personally leading the pursuit, Tafoya directed Deputy Tom Curtis to form a posse. Some disagreement exists about the composition of this body of lawmen. Oscar Caudill alleged that it consisted of twelve or fourteen men, that they were not a legally constituted posse, and that they had no arrest warrant. George Curry relates that the posse consisted of only four men, headed by John Cox, Henry Coleman's old friend. Cox had been a bondsman for Coleman. When the outlaw jumped his bond, Cox evidently felt relieved of any obligation to the fugitive. In his recollections of this unfortunate affair, Cox says that Deputy Curtis asked him to join the posse. Cox agreed on the condition that Curtis not permit Coleman to retain a weapon after arrest. When the posse approached Coleman's ranch, he attempted to escape and was shot. He bled to death in a ditch near his home. Cox believed that posseman Jim Cheetham fired the fatal bullet, but an autopsy subsequently pointed to Cox's rifle as the lethal weapon. Friends of the dead man attempted to obtain an indictment of John Cox and the other possemen, but failed.[143]

The deputies then summoned a local justice of the peace to conduct a coroner's inquest. In a strange turn of events—although not so uncommon in the frontier conditions still prevailing in western Socorro County—the justice was H. H. Lyle, victim of Coleman's last cattle raid. The inquest was a crude affair. "They drug [sic] him [Coleman] outa that ditch where they had him," recalled John Cox, and the judge—an avid card player—looked upon the corpse of the badman and reflected, "'I never saw an ace in the hole that was any prettier than that sonofabitch dead."[144]

The Henry Coleman case was just one of several troublesome issues that arose in Elfego Baca's shrievalty. In November 1919, six bandits attacked the residence of Abran Contreras, a wealthy rancher who resided some six miles from La Joya. The thugs severely wounded him in the arm, which later had to be amputated, in an effort to make him divulge the whereabouts of his money. Contreras refused to use banks and reportedly kept up to $20,000 hidden on the premises. The outlaws brought a supply of dynamite with which to blow up the house, in order to uncover the money. The barking of a dog frightened the thieves, who fled before locating the cash.[145]

Sheriff Baca and four deputies were soon on the trail of the outlaws in the Manzano Mountains. Baca insisted that his office handle the case and rejected an offer of assistance from the New Mexico Mounted Police. The sheriff quickly divined that the band consisted of locals rather than outsiders. If a group of strangers had entered his county, Baca would soon learn about them. The lawman and his subordinates began to collect evidence, to include a poorly disguised horse and some aromatic bits of human refuse left by the highwaymen at one of their camps. When the trail of the outlaws led to the remote mountain community of Manzano, the villagers were very hostile and refused to assist the officers. Baca persisted with his search and soon located two suspects, Pedro Sais and Luciano Padilla, barricaded in a house. To prompt their surrender, the sheriff threatened to dynamite the structure with the very explosives that the robbers had left at the scene of their crime. Baca later declared that he eventually arrested all of the highwaymen, except one man who escaped to Mexico where he was killed.[146]

Elfego Baca's term in the sheriff's office took place in an age of transition for both criminals and lawmen. The introduction of the telephone and the automobile were especially important. During the World War I era, long distance telephone calls became possible in New Mexico, and automobile transportation was rapidly becoming a necessity. In 1916, only three years before Elfego Baca became sheriff, Congress initiated a system of United States highways for the entire nation. At the same time, New Mexicans were pressing for the improvement of local roads. The prospects of a lucrative tourist trade loomed. In August 1919, the businessmen of Albuquerque estimated that as many as 7,000 automobiles would pass through their community in the summer alone, en route to the scenic Southwest. In this same year Socorrans were surprised to learn that their community was under consideration as a stopover for a nationwide commercial airline, and an aircraft was scheduled for a trial landing there.[147]

But the automobile proved to be the most pressing problem for Sheriff Elfego Baca and his colleagues in other counties. Car theft rings began to flourish. In July 1919, Albuquerque officers arrested two thieves and recovered a Stutz automobile that had been taken in California. An automobile club in that state had alerted the New Mexico lawmen about it. The felons not only had spare license plates, but dies for making new ones. In the following October, three men stole an automobile in Holbrook, Ariozna, looted a store, and fled into Sheriff Elfego Baca's bailiwick. Navajo County Sheriff C. W. Harp trailed the bandits as far as Magdalena where he gave up the chase. Whether Baca managed to capture these new-styled outlaws is not known. He later recollected the case of a man who had stolen an automobile in Las Cruces and fled northward. Elfego took up the chase in a car—a far cry from his past horseback pursuits—and eventually brought the thief to a halt with a chance pistol shot through the gas tank of the felon's vehicle.[148]

Sheriff Baca earned some adverse publicity in a case of car theft in September 1919. When four men dressed in army uniforms, presumably veterans, stole a Ford automobile in Albuquerque and fled southward, Bernalillo County Sheriff Rafael Garcia alerted Elfego Baca. Baca arrested the suspects and took custody of the car. When Deputy Sheriff Charles Banghart and J. M. Boyd, owner of the stolen vehicle, traveled to Socorro, lawman Baca refused to turn over either prisoners or automobile until they paid a bill for twenty-five-dollars for the sheriff's services. When they protested "that the high cost of arrests was exorbitant," according to an Albuquerque journalist, Baca haughtily replied that he would retain "automobile and boys [prisoners] and all, in his hands rather than come down on the price." Sheriff Garcia was outraged and characterized his Socorro County colleague's charges as "another case of profiteering." While the reason for Elfego's charges in this case was not explained, the Albuquerque officers probably assumed that the Socorro County board of supervisors would pay Baca for his expenses, as in all such matters. It is not clear what Elfego Baca's rationale was for this twenty-five-dollar fee or how the case was eventually resolved. The Albuquerque newspaper reported that the four prisoners were in the Socorro County lockup for at least thirty days, "and there's no telling how long the car will stay."[149]

These mysterious expenses for the car thieves and stolen automobile may have been related to another issue that Elfego Baca later described. Prior to his entry into the sheriff's office, Socorro

County had been constrained to rent warehouse space at $100 per month in order to shelter official vehicles and property impounded by the sheriff's office. The twenty-five dollar fee that the peace officer imposed upon the Boyd vehicle may have been for such services. As Baca explained, he

> saw that he could build a garage with the prisoners and started to build one. He built a garage estimated to the value of $8,000.00, and to build same he decided on the following plan: To arrest all tramps and put them to work on the garage. Among those caught were stonemasons, adobemakers, adobe-layers, plasterers, carpenters, and painters.

"Said building is still standing," Elfego proudly reminded voters in subsequent electioneering.[150]

Elfego Baca demonstrated a spirit of independence in the sheriff's office that recalled his frontier predecessors in the days of Pedro Simpson. Forty years earlier, the chief county lawmen performed their duties with few legislative restraints. In his role as jailer, Baca took liberties that brought him into conflicts with other officials. When a new and more stringent debtor law forced the sheriff to arrest many poor sheepherders, who often went into debt as a consequence of their seasonal occupation, Baca reacted angrily to what he believed was an unjust statute that benefited only the wealthy sheep raisers. The Socorro County jail soon housed eleven victims of this unwise legislation, each of whom was sentenced to sixty days at public expense. Baca resolved this dilemma by arbitrarily liberating them, over the objections of District Attorney Harry Owen. While Baca admitted that he was placing himself in jeopardy, his decision was eventually vindicated when the legislature repealed the debtor law. On another occasion this impetuous lawman assigned a jail inmate, Joseph Fisher, the task of running down a comrade named Watson, who had escaped Baca's carcel. Baca insisted that this highly unorthodox method was successful, although he experienced some anxious moments as he awaited the results.[151]

In spite of his seemingly flippant conduct of office, the Socorro County sheriff took his position seriously. He played a prominent part in the New Mexico Sheriffs and Peace Officers' Association, being elected to a five year term on the board of directors at its February meeting in 1919. This gathering entertained several important matters. Some fears had been expressed that the lawmen opposed the re-creation of the Mounted Police and, in the words of one journalist, "would start a war" against these state officers. (The mounties had been abolished in 1910, then resurrected at private expense in 1918). The association resolved to support the Mounted Police as long as they were "under proper regulations." They also discussed the difficulties attending the enforcement of the new dry law and the detection of automobile thieves. In connection with the latter problem, the peace officers requested legislation requiring every garage and auto mechanic to keep accurate records about every transient vehicle that was serviced.[152]

The presence of all twenty-eight of New Mexico's sheriffs, among them Elfego Baca, at this Santa Fe meeting was a cause for comment. When many of them boarded the train at Lamy Junction, near the capital, for points south, the *Albuquerque Evening Herald* reported that a porter on the train was momentarily taken aback. "Fo' de Lawd's sake," he exclaimed, "dar shore must be some hoss thieves loose in this here country." W. C. Simpson, sheriff of Luna County, agreed with the porter, but in a subsequent interview in Albuquerque, assured the citizenry that the peace officers "are going to run them down." Simpson added that he had "never seen a more efficient list of sheriffs, or men who are more in earnest in their work. . . .There is a general feeling in the association that the time has come for sheriffs to stop being politicians and become aggressive law officers."[153]

Elfego Baca enjoyed the prestige that the Socorro County sheriff's office brought him. He found it "was a sensation to be remembered." He recalled that he "put his feet upon the desk . . . and accepted the homage of his henchmen." The public recognized his position in various ways. Abe B. Baca, Elfego's nephew, who remembered his uncle's term as sheriff, said that "he would walk every day from the courthouse to the post office. . . .On the way back he would stop at Judge Green's bar. The judge would give him a toddy." While such conduct might appear arrogant to some citizens, Elfego Baca did not necessarily intend it to appear so. Abe Baca believed that Elfego exhibited many good attributes:

> My uncle was a good man. He didn't abuse his authority He liked kids, old folks and animals. And he had a good sense of humor.[154]

Whatever his good intentions, Elfego Baca aroused some passionate opposition during his two-year term. George Curry, Baca's political nemesis in the 1912 congressional race, was very critical of the sheriff's cavalier treatment of prisoners such as Henry Coleman. Such opposition angered the sheriff, recalled Curry, and Elfego Baca "became my personal and political enemy." When the Socorro County Republican Party convention met in Magdalena in 1920, Elfego Baca won renomination to the post. He then led the fight in Socorro County for the renomination of his friend, Octaviano A. Larrazolo, as governor of New Mexico. At the subsequent state convention, George Curry opposed Larrazolo. Curry believed that the former governor had committed too many indiscretions, including pardoning Mexican revolutionaries who were serving terms in the state penitentiary. Curry joined Holm O. Bursum, one of the most influential Republicans in the state, to propose the name of Merrit Mechem. Elfego Baca flew into a rage. "I clashed with Elfego Baca on the convention floor," admitted Curry, "in an exchange which all but led to blows." Mechem won the nomination and Baca had another grudge to add to his personal blacklist against George Curry.[155]

Elfego Baca did not take criticism and defeat lightly. As Curry recalled, the confrontation on the convention floor "had its repercussions when we returned home to Socorro county." The sheriff refused to support Merrit Mechem for governor and persisted in leading his followers into the Larrazolo camp. Curry directed the campaign for Mechem in the county, while Bursum did the same at the state level. In order to win the western precincts of Socorro County for Mechem, George Curry promised them a county of their own. Curry recalled that the region was growing, with many new farmers and cattlemen settling there. The fact that they were Democrats did not dissuade him. Curry thought it "politically expedient" as a means to win more votes for his candidate. Elfego Baca regarded this tactic as a stab in the back from a fellow Republican. Furthermore, the formation of a new county would reduce the size of his shrievalty. Curry admitted that some persons criticized him by pointing to the lack of population and tax base in the western end of the county, but such remarks were to no avail. In November 1920, Merrit Mechem won the governorship and the new county, Catron, was created in the following year. By this time, Elfego Baca was no longer sheriff, having lost his bid for re-election.[156]

As the 1920 campaign heated up in the fall, Elfego Baca sensed that the odds were growing against him. His maverick-like position within the Republican Party no doubt hurt his chances. George Curry recalled a visit by the sheriff and two other men, Deputy Al Woods and Luther Foster, a local butcher whom many regarded as a bad man. Foster approached Curry at his hotel desk. "Governor, I'd like to have a private talk with you," said Foster, "Come outside where we can talk." Curry immediately sensed danger. Baca and Woods stood some distance away in the lobby, with the deputy behind his boss. But Curry believed he could plainly see Woods, whom the hotel man regarded as a friend, give a sign confirming his fear that Baca and Foster posed a threat. Curry pulled a shotgun from under his desk and replied, "If you are hunting trouble, start it here or get out." After a tense moment, Baca said to Foster, "Come on." The sheriff walked away with his two gunsels in tow. Al Woods soon turned in his badge and Luther Foster was convicted of a murder and sentenced to prison.[157]

Whether Elfego Baca truly intended more than to scare George Curry is difficult to determine. As the 1920 election campaign drew to a close, Elfego Baca apparently had a change of heart and concluded that party unity was essential to his political future. When Albert B. Fall announced plans to speak in Socorro on behalf of Warren G. Harding, the Republican presidential candidate, Baca saw an opportunity to win laurels and possibly to entertain Fall. The sheriff "sent his chief deputy to me," recalled George Curry, "with a message of peace and asking to see me." Curry consented. At their meeting, Baca indicated a desire to support "the entire Republican ticket." "We shook hands," wrote Curry, "and our private war ended."[158]

After a decade of confrontation with Elfego Baca, George Curry probably knew his adversary very well. As a veteran sheriff, Curry had become acquainted with many tough and belligerent men. He paid homage to Elfego Baca's reputation for courage by admitting that this Hispano leader's "threat of violence always merited careful consideration." The upshot of the campaign of 1920 was a general victory for the Republican ticket across the state, with the notable exception of Elfego Baca. He lost his bid for reelection to the shrievalty. The residents of western Socorro County received their new county, Catron, in the following year. Reserve, formerly Upper San Francisco Plaza, the place where Baca's career began, became the county seat. It was perhaps fitting that one of the last of the overgrown frontier counties, Socorro, was divided as one of the last frontier lawmen, Elfego Baca, passed from the sheriff's office.[159]

Baca enjoyed publicizing himself as a two-gun man late in life. (Photo courtesy Museum of New Mexico).

CHAPTER SIX

A CHAMPION OF THE PEOPLE

The loss of the sheriff's race apparently persuaded Elfego Baca to seek opportunities elsewhere, in Mexico. He informed his biographer that he obtained a job as chief bouncer for the Tivoli Gambling Hall, just across the border in Ciudad Juarez. He told the *Socorro Chieftain*, in June 1921, that he was then "holding a lucrative position with the Mexican government in Juarez." While he did not elaborate, the position of Tivoli bouncer may have been a government post. Mexico City awarded concessions to gambling establishments. Elfego looked back upon this position as one of his best. He earned $750 per month and directed a large staff.[160]

While working at the Tivoli, Elfego had occasion to meet Mary Garden, a famous soprano and director of the Chicago Grand Opera. This encounter between the internationally renowned singer and the western gunfighter took place in the spring of 1921. The *New York Times* noted that the Chicago Grand Opera Company was scheduled to depart on a western tour on 7 March and return to Chicago in May. Garden and members of her troupe patronized the Tivoli and had a "jolly" time, according to Baca. In fact, when she won at roulette, "the scene threatened to become riotous," at which point the chief bouncer was constrained to ask Garden and her followers "to be a little less noisy." Far from being antagonized, the famous singer invited Baca to her hotel and gave him a ticket to her next performance of "Carmen." While Elfego Baca was sufficiently impressed with Mary Garden's fame to arrange to be photographed with her, he admitted that he did not enjoy "all that hollering around." "I like the Mexican string bands better," he said. In *Mary Garden's Story*, she recalled touring the West but failed to mention a stopover in El Paso. She did remember singing in another Texas community, Dallas, under conditions that were "very primitive."[161]

Elfego Baca's fortunes changed rapidly in the early 1920s. Within weeks of his relocation to Ciudad Juarez, he was called away on a new adventure. Albert B. Fall, United States senator from New Mexico, had recently resigned his seat to become President Warren G. Harding's secretary of Interior in early 1921. Baca had enjoyed a cordial relationship with this powerful Democrat-turned-Republican since Fall's campaign for the United States Senate in 1912. Elfego later claimed that his entrapment of the four state legislators in the scheme to sell their votes to the highest bidder in a senatorial race had ensured Fall's election. This longstanding friendship bore fruit for Elfego in the form of an appointment as an Indian and land inspector for the Interior Department. Baca traveled to the national capital some weeks later, in July 1921, to visit the new cabinet member. While there, he stopped by the White House to personally express his appreciation to President Harding for the appointment of his patron to the secretaryship.[162]

One of Elfego's first duties as Interior Department agent was to investigate an Indian problem in remote southeastern Utah. In May 1921, Paiutes and white ranchers clashed near Bluff. In an effort to arrest Chief Joe Dutchups and his followers for cattle theft, a sheriff's posse fired on the natives. Dutchups was wounded and taken into custody. When his angry followers began to cut telephone lines and burn bridges, alarmed homesteaders and forest rangers fled to nearby towns. The United States marshal and Utah National Guard were alerted. A conference between local officials and tribal leaders at Blanding ended without agreement, and the Indians were reported as "sulky." Interior Secretary Fall decided to dispatch Elfego Baca to the scene. Fall's assistants expressed some fear that one man—this "gentleman of fair rotundity and a mild, humorous countenance" —

would be killed. According to Elfego, the Secretary replied confidently, "You save your sympathies for the Paiutes."[163]

This assignment proved to be very difficult. Not only was the disturbed region in an out-of-the-way place, but heavy rains fell in southeastern Utah. Baca arrived in Salt Lake on 24 August but telegraphed Secretary Fall on 1 September that he had been unable to make the trip. The roads to Bluff were "in [an] impassible condition," he said. This delay enabled Elfego to gather information about the Indian problem. In a letter to Theodore Mack, secretary to Fall, the inspector assured him that "I am satisfied that when I make my final report the Secretary of Interior will be more than pleased to have put me in charge of this investigation." He expected the trip to take as much as fifteen days. Unfortunately, Elfego neglected to provide details about this mission, except to say that he brought the Indian culprits "to time" and that the people of Utah were grateful for his services. By 16 September he was back in Salt Lake City and awaiting documents in another case. His term as a government inspector may have lasted only a few months, since Albert Fall resigned in March 1923 under a cloud of suspicion of having used his position for personal gain. Fall was subsequently sent to prison for having accepted bribes to illegally lease federal oil lands in the Teapot Dome Scandal.[164]

This expose dismayed Elfego Baca and the many supporters of Albert Fall in New Mexico. Baca accompanied a delegation to the national capital to lobby on behalf of the fallen politico. Baca fails to mention the origins of his association with this ambitious man, but admits that both of them were educated in the "harsh political school" of territorial politics. Fall was "dynamic, ruthless, [and] overwhelming," recalled Baca, and he wielded an "uncanny sway over the native vote." When he jumped the Democratic traces and joined the Republicans, many of his followers did likewise. He demanded absolute loyalty. "It was this code that applied to Elfego Baca," he said, "and every other loyal Republican." In 1928, when Baca made these observations to Kyle Crichton, he still expressed "bewilderment at the roar of the press" against Albert Fall. At the same time, he realized that Fall's motto—"Anything for a friend; to hell with our enemies"—was difficult for most people to accept. In New Mexico, continued this veteran Spanish-American politician, "It is the world of political favors, of expediency, [and] of 'loyalty'" that makes the system function. He blamed this corruption of the political system upon the generous distribution of money by such wealthy magnates as William F. "Bull" Andrews, rather than the relatively poor Albert Fall. Such a cynical assessment was no doubt connected to the decline of Elfego's political fortunes after the humiliation of his patron. While many New Mexicans continued to hold Baca in high regard, they ceased to bestow public offices upon him. One of his last official positions was that of Bernalillo County jailer, a rather lowly task when measured against his past accomplishments.[165]

Elfego Baca lived out his remaining years in Albuquerque and sought to rebuild his faltering career. These efforts were difficult at best, since he sometimes drank to excess and was constrained to take the embarrassing measure of declaring bankruptcy in 1924. These problems no doubt contributed to the estrangement of his wife, Frances. Robert Hoath LaFollette, who opened a law practice in Albuquerque in 1926, recalled that Mrs. Baca retained him and his partner, M. Ralph Brown, about this time. The estranged wife, who resided in California, complained that her husband had failed to make payments for her support, as the court ordered. With the proper papers filed, the case came up for a hearing, wrote LaFollette:

> We arrived at the courthouse a little before two. As we drove up, we saw a large limousine pull up and a ferocious-looking man step out, with a bodyguard. Mr. Brown called my attention to the fact that we could distinctly see the impression of pistols on their hips. After we had the citation issued, we had received 'grapevine' information to the effect that we were up against one of the real bad-men of the Southwest, and we were prepared to fight accordingly.

Much to the young lawyers' relief, Elfego merely requested the assurance of the judge that Frances Baca's attorneys were duly licensed. Baca then explained "that he was sick and was having great difficulties," recalled LaFollette, "and the Court took the matter under advisement with [the] admonishment that Mr. Baca attempt in the near future to pay up the arrears."[166]

Although the two Bacas were eventually reunited in Albuquerque, their relationship continued to be rather stormy. While "they did not exactly live happily ever afterward," wrote William A. Keleher, "they lived together as husband and wife." Baca unwittingly contributed to this familial friction by combining his law office and residence in one building at the corner of Sixth Street and Gold Avenue. He complained that she failed to respect his official privacy and sometimes interrupted conferences with clients. "She never knocked on the door marked, 'Private,' before entering," Baca informed Keleher. This domestic strife reached the boiling point when Baca asked Keleher to draw up a complaint and ask the court for a restraining order against the intrusive spouse. As a friend, Keleher recommended against this extreme measure, pointing out that the public would look upon this as incongruous. "Many people will be unable to understand how it comes that you [a famous gunfighter] are unable to handle Mrs. Baca," argued the attorney. Elfego replied rather dejectedly, "You just don't know Mrs. Baca."[167]

Elfego Baca continued to support causes that he considered worthy. In 1928 he journeyed to the nation's capital to lobby for a bill to create the Middle Rio Grande Conservancy District. Although he overstated his contribution to this controversial bill, Baca was able to approach Senator Charles Curtis of Kansas (the Vice President-elect), who could play an important role in breaking the deadlock in Congress. The two had played together as boys in Topeka, Kansas, and had remained friends. After talking over old times, Curtis proposed a means to win passage of the bill. It became law on 22 December 1927.[168]

Elfego Baca continued to seek political office, but without success. This misfortune was, in part, a consequence of the peculiarly unstable nature of New Mexico politics, as well as Baca's independent spirit. In 1924 he made an unsuccessful bid for the judgeship of the Second Disrict, which included Bernalillo and Sandoval counties. True to his maverick-like personality, he deserted the Republican Party and ran as an independent. As a campaign measure, he distributed an autobiographical sketch that has served as a basis for much of the inflated and often erroneous information that continues to circulate about him. He also joined a local reform ticket, the Law and Order League. This is the source of the title of the Baca story, *Law and Order, Ltd.*, which appeared in 1928. In that year, he again entered the race for Bernalillo County sheriff. To promote this campaign, he organized the Elfego Baca Bolt & Nut Club, which reportedly enrolled several hundred members. He also edited the club newspaper, *La Tuerica* (The Nut). As a means of demonstrating his qualifications for office, he staged a shooting demonstration one afternoon at an Albuquerque nightclub, in which he shot off the heads of twenty chickens! Such trick shooting might have impressed oldtimers, but not the younger generation which voted in opposition.[169]

It was probably with a view to furthering his political fortunes that Elfego Baca sought a biographer. In 1927 he approached William A. Keleher, who refused the undertaking but recommended Kyle S. Crichton. Although the latter writer accepted, he soon expressed serious misgivings to Keleher. With only half of the manuscript completed, Baca already boasted seven notches on his gun. "I am afraid he will go on a rampage . . . and murder me," explained Crichton, "if I make him out in the book as a bad man." On the contrary, replied Keleher, Baca would take it as a slight if the author "failed to hold him out to the public as a first class gunman, and a more than typical bad man of the Southwest." With this reassurance, Crichton completed the story; however, *Law and Order, Ltd., The Rousing Life of Elfego Baca of New Mexico* can hardly be called biography. It is, as historian Ralph H. Vigil observed, "a strange mixture of fact, fancy, and pictorial imagination." Crichton made no effort to document the important events in his subject's life, although it is entertaining reading as it stands. In the absence of serious editing, the book approximates an autobiography and is valuable for Elfego Baca's account of some events in his life. As Keleher points out, Bronson Cutting, one of Baca's patrons, probably underwrote some of the publication expense. Cutting's newspaper, the *Daily New Mexican*, published the book. Baca naturally enjoyed this attention and once expressed the hope to George Baldwin of the *Albuquerque Tribune* that Hollywood would make a movie of his life.[170]

In 1930 Elfego Baca made the final break with the GOP and joined the Democrats. Trace jumping was not uncommon in the jumbled politics of New Mexico in the post-World War I era. By this time, Baca had joined the ranks of the rising political star in New Mexico, Bronson Cutting. A wealthy New Yorker and a member of a liberal Republican family, Cutting had purchased the Santa Fe *Daily New Mexican*. With this leading statewide journal at his command, Cutting became the most influential maverick Republican in New Mexico. The Hispanic population, including Elfego Baca, soon joined the Cutting movement. Not only did the New Yorker introduce American Legion posts as a means to marshal a following, but Baca complemented them with "independent progressive Republican clubs." Baca's Spanish-language newspaper, *La Opinion Publica*, also supported Cutting. Although the two politicos did not move in the same social circles, the aristocratic newspaperman appreciated the abilities of the veteran gunman-politician in the field. Cutting even suggested through the columns of his newspaper Elfego Baca's name as potential governor material, which was the latter's dream as a capstone to his career. Whether the editor was truly serious or was merely giving him "honorable mention" as a ritualistic concession to his Hispanic following is not clear. If so, Baca would probably have sensed this vicious tactic, having had a similar experience in his bid for the congressional seat in 1912. Whatever the case, this alliance failed to advance Baca's career.[171]

The association of Bronson Cutting with Elfego Baca was much closer than many New Mexicans realized. This fact emerged in an unusual way. On 6 May 1935 Cutting, now United States senator, was killed in a plane crash in Missouri. In the course of settling the Cutting estate, his administrators brought suit against Elfego Baca's office building in Albuquerque. The heirs alleged that Cutting had acquired title by assuming debts against the building some years earlier. Baca retained the law firm of William A. Keleher and countered with a claim of $44,000 for services provided to Cutting as a private detective. This news startled many prominent politicians who desired to know more. An Albuquerque dispatch of 4 June 1936 reported that "Baca contended the Senator had agreed to pay him $5000 for eight years, thereby cancelling the mortgage" on the Albuquerque property. Among the persons whom Baca had investigated for Senator Cutting were former Governor Octaviano Larrazolo, former Senator Holm O. Bursum, and others. These surreptitious activities had gone on between 1924 and 1934. To prove his point, recalled Keleher, Baca wisely retained "carbon copies of the numerous letters and reports . . . containing detailed information on political affairs in New Mexico" that he had mailed to Senator Cutting in Washington. Such news caused considerable fretting among prominent persons not only in the state but within the Cutting family, who directed that an out-of-court settlement be arranged. Elfego Baca received clear title to his property on 6 January 1937.[172]

The old campaigner was a clever man and possessed insights into the voting drives of his constituency. In March 1938, Baca asked that William A. Keleher drive him to Magdalena, the purpose being to enable the aging politico to purchase the wooden figure of *Mi Senora Santa Ana*. A legend, cleverly aided and abetted by Elfego, had arisen around this *santo* to the effect that she alone had survived unscathed the Frisco Plaza siege with Baca in 1884. Baca claimed that "he had hugged her close and she kept him safe." He had sought this prized relic for many years and planned to take it on a lecture tour of New Mexico. Not only would he be able to recall his more glorious days, but Baca, the experienced vote getter, would no doubt derive political value as well. Unfortunately, the owner of the *santo* refused to accept Elfego's promissory note for five hundred dollars and the deal fell through.[173]

Baca assumed a fallback position. He had his photograph taken with the *santo* and circulated copies during his future political campaigns. One print went to Archbishop R. A. Gerken in Santa Fe, along with a copy of the Crichton biography. On 21 March, his excellency responded in a letter mixed with humor and concern for Elfego's spiritual well-being. After thanking him for the book, which "one of the old fathers is reading now," Father Gerken continued:

> I also want to thank you for the fine picture of yourself and Santana, the latter being over 500 years old and the former 73. It is a fine match . . . and a fine picture all

the way round. One of course may be more distinguished for sanctity but I am sure the other is more distinguished for his law and order reputation.

The concerned archbishop could not pass up the opportunity to urge Baca, whose religious life was notably in question, to attend Sunday services. "I would feel especially proud if you would give me an opportunity to give you Holy Communion," he wrote.[174]

Elfego Baca continued to seek the mandate of the people throughout his declining years. On 1 January 1934, he had announced his candidacy for the governorship of New Mexico. He released a manifesto of nineteen points that he regarded as essential for the welfare of his state. Ever the lawman at heart, he devoted much of this list to the betterment of law enforcement. In this automobile age, "too many outlaws come and go," he said. In his nineteenth point, he promised to pardon a penitentiary inmate on "each and every Saturday." Not only were the 600 prisoners in the state prison an enormous expense, but he believed that a majority "have been convicted because they did not have the proper defense." His failure to win the governorship merely caused him to redouble his efforts to gain higher office. When a Works Projects Administration writer interviewed him in July 1936, Baca had just decided to run for district judge. He reissued the *Political Record* from an earlier race and averred that he would perform his judicial duties "without taking into consideration politics, nationality or religion." In spite of his failure in this campaign, he made another unsuccessful bid for the judgeship four years later. In an "Open Letter" to the public on 4 November 1940, he thanked the nearly 4,000 persons who voted for him and took pride in the fact that they cast their ballots for him "without any [monetary] compensation."[175]

Elfego Baca exhibited an admirable lust for life and proved to be a very durable man. Donald Eklund, a native of Albuquerque, recalled seeing him regularly in the early 1940s when delivering newspapers to Baca's office. Although he did not take many cases, the attorney still exhibited his shingle over "a small, nondescript" office across from the Packard automobile dealership. In his abrupt manner, the old gunfighter gruffly demanded that the newsboy stop, get off his bicycle, and carefully place the paper between the screen door and the main door. It was not uncommon to see Baca in his office at 5:30 a. m. On some occasions, recalled Eklund, Baca would be playing the fiddle and dancing! The absence of a partner did not discourage him. Eklund remembered that the grey-haired Baca would be "jumping around and having a good time," and although in his late seventies, was still "a wiry old guy."[176]

Elfego Baca enjoyed letter writing and maintained a large circle of correspondents. He composed epistles "on every conceivable subject," according to writer George Fitzpatrick. Although he feared that his command of the English was faulty, his letters often contained touches of charm and, as always, good humor. As his seventy-seventh birthday approached, he urged a good friend to pay him a visit:

> I would like to have a talk with you and [know] when you intend to come, write to me two days ahead so I will known you are coming, so you and I can have a real Mexican dinner.

When a fellow attorney made remarks on the radio that Elfego and Frances enjoyed, he complimented the barrister:

> We heard your talk on the radio last night and it was good. Congratulations—Shake.[177]

When radio man Bob Ripley featured Elfego Baca on the "Believe It Or Not" program—a distinction that must have especially gratified him—the flattered gunman wrote the *Daily New Mexican* for more copies of the photo showing Baca with his radio host:

> *Estimado Amigo* :
> A pretty girl passed by my office door today at 3 p.m. and she showed me a picture of Bob Ripley and I, taken on the 24th of May, 1940. She took the picture with her. Will you please send me a copy of this paper? . . . Tell them you will be my security until I pay the bill.[178]

Long before Baca's death, he had begun to enter the realm of legend. The body of apocryphal stories about him continues to grow. In November 1907, the *Southwestern Miller*, a trade journal in St. Paul, Minnesota, published sketches about several New Mexico characters, among them Elfego Baca. Eugene Manlove Rhodes contributed to the growth of the myth when he included Baca in a novelette, *Hit the Line Hard*. The author calls his subject Octaviano Baca, but has him serving as the district attorney for Socorro. This elevation of Elfego Baca to legendary status was completed in the 1920s when popular writers began to "deify" other frontier characters such as Wyatt Earp. James H. Cook and William French published their versions of the San Francisco Plaza fight in 1923 and 1927, respectively. Elfego Baca's autobiographical sketch appeared in 1924. He enlarged upon this sometimes fanciful story through Kyle Crichton's biographical attempt in 1928. As writer Erna Fergusson observes, Baca "told his own tale," and Crichton "wrote it down for him."[179]

Other writers soon began to broadcast these firsthand accounts more widely. B. A. Botkin included Crichton's rendition of "the siege of Elfego Baca" by Texas cowboys in the popular *A Treasury of Western Folklore* in 1951. The ultimate apotheosis of Elfego Baca took place seven years later with the translation of this famous Hispano character onto the Hollywood screen. "The Nine Lives of Elfego Baca," by Walt Disney Productions, recounted his exploits at San Francisco Plaza and followed the Baca-Crichton version of his subsequent life very closely. At the end of the movie, Baca (played by Robert Loggia) boards a stagecoach in Socorro for Santa Fe where he plans to study law and to defend his people through the courts against unjust Anglo interlopers. This growing body of legend and misinformation is supplemented by a popular song, "The Ballad of Elfego," and the discovery of relics associated with him. A pair of rusty six-shooters marked "E. B." was reportedly found under his old office building in Albuquerque. Socorrans hold an annual golf tournament called the *Elfego Baca Shoot*, described as "a difficult, different and memorable event, quite like the life and times of the man." The reason for this assertion is that the participants tee off from the top of Socorro Peak, at 7,243 feet above sea level. Elfego Baca would be delighted at this odd form of recognition.[180]

Western buffs measure the fame of a frontier gunfighter by the number of men he killed. To have several lethal events knotched on his gun—to have "killed his man" in frontier parlance—placed the gunman in a distinguished, if dubious, category. Elfego Baca claimed to have killed nine men, although evidence is lacking. He participated in several shootouts where the firing was general. In such encounters Elfego could not legitimately claim to have inflicted the fatal wounds. This was probably the case in the shooting of cowboy Townsend at Escondido in 1883. It is certain that bullets from his gun, fired blindly through a door, ended the life of Bert Hearne in San Francisco Plaza. Baca's gun contributed only indirectly to the death of Young Parham, whose injured horse fell on his rider and caused mortal injuries. Baca did kill Celestino Otero. Donald Eklund, the former newspaper boy, recalled that his father told about seeing Baca kill a man in Socorro during World War I; however, this incident is unconfirmed and may be a corruption of the El Paso shooting. The facts attribute only two deaths directly to Elfego Baca's gun. Certainly he retained a cautious and wary air about him throughout his life.[181]

Elfego Baca occupies a prominent place in Southwestern legend and many Hispanos regard him as a pioneer leader of the resistance to the American intrusion into nineteenth century New Mexico. As Carey McWilliams, a student of this clash between ethnic groups, observed, Baca's stand against the Texas cowboys in San Francisco Plaza in 1884 had considerable influence. The young Hispano deputy "demonstrated that New Mexicans could shoot as accurately as Texans," concluded McWilliams. But this scholar exaggerates when he adds that "the encroachment of Texas folkways in New Mexico came to a dead halt" after this event. Kyle Crichton asserts that "The chief significance of Elfego Baca is that he has been able to meet and hold his own with the Anglo at his own game."[182]

Historian Robert J. Rosenbaum places Elfego Baca more incongruously in the genre of the social bandit, the lawbreaker whom members of his race often shield from lawmen, who are usually members of an alien group. Rosenbaum does not intend to convey the impression that Baca was clearly an outlaw, but he ranks him with outlaws Vicente Silva, Jose Chavez y Chavez, and Juan de Dios Ortega, as individuals who refused to submit to Anglo oppression. Rosenbaum is aware that the facts of Baca's life have been embellished and declares that one unnamed New Mexico writer called him "that fat fraud." This scholar correctly asserts that Baca "is now among the ranks of *mexicano* heroes." Baca would be pleased, and his biographer rightly asserted of him that, "from his earliest days [he] has been the idol and the protector of the less fortunate members of his race."[183]

While such speculation may have some basis in fact, Elfego Baca's place in New Mexican history is nonetheless equivocal. In spite of his professed desire to assist the Hispanic people, they did not always return the favor. His loss of elections in Socorro and Bernalillo counties—regions of considerable Spanish-American populations—attest to this fact. His countrymen may have considered him to be *agringado*, or Anglicized, after the fashion of other ambitious native New Mexicans, such as Miguel A. Otero, Jr., a contemporary and governor of New Mexico Territory at the turn of the century. Baca admitted that residence for his first fifteen years in Topeka, Kansas, rendered him more at ease with the English language than with his native tongue. The ease with which he entered the ranks of Anglo members of the New Mexico bar confirmed this fact. But such speculation can be carried too far. Baca maintained close attachments to his fellow Hispanics through the *Hispania Americana Alianza* throughout his life and rose to high position in this organization. Indeed, if the legend reflects any degree of truth, it still places him clearly within the ranks of New Mexico Hispanos.[184]

After some eighty eventful years, Elfego Baca died on 27 August 1945. Although he had been in declining health for some years, he had continued to think and act politics. In June of the previous year, he had again announced his candidacy for the position of district attorney. "My friends have asked me" to run, he said in the by now familiar *Political Record* which he had issued in many campaigns. His good friend Robert LaFollette financed a radio spot for the tireless campaigner. Indeed, for Elfego Baca politics, not guns, were his first love, as William A. Keleher has noted. Frances Pohmer Baca, Elfego's wife of sixty years, informed New Mexico Congressman Clinton P. Anderson that her husband passed away as he sat by the radio waiting "to hear you speak over the air." As his obituary notice observed, his many years of public service "marked him as a unique champion of the Spanish-American people." He fought "their battles with law-books as zestfully as he ever fought them with rifle and revolver." He would also have taken pride in the fact that the *New York Times* reprinted his obituary, one that reflected the traditionally overblown version of his life. Services were held at the Immaculate Conception Church, the Reverend Patrick J. Keleher presiding. The announcement, which was widely circulated, included verses from Alfred Lord Tennyson's poem, "Crossing the Bar." Elfego Baca was laid to rest in Sunset Memorial Park, in Albuquerque, New Mexico.[185]

NOTES

[1]The literature about Elfego Baca is voluminous, but derives from *Political Record of Elfego Baca and A Brief History of His Life*, issued in 1924 to promote Baca's candicacy for district attorney of the Second Judicial District. This item is available in Tom Vinegar's lightly annotated *Here Comes Elfego! The Autobiography of Elfego Baca* (Albuquerque: Vinegar Tom, n. d.), 22 pp. Later printings (1940 and 1944) of the *Political Record* in and Spanish and English language versions are located in the Elfego Baca Papers, Special Collections Department, Zimmerman Library, University of New Mexico, Albuquerque. Much of this collection was stolen some years ago. Kyle S. Crichton's *Law and Order, Ltd.: The Rousing Life of Elfego Baca of New Mexico* (1928; reprint, Glorieta, N. Mex.: Rio Grande Press, 1970) approximates an autobiography of Elfego Baca. Crichton performed very little research but permitted Baca to tell his own story.

The popular literature about Elfego Baca is extensive, but seldom goes beyond his own recollections and Crichton's biography. Among recent treatments are Leon Claire Metz, *The Shooters* (El Paso: Mangan Books, 1976), 75-80; Byron A. Johnson, "The Rousing Life of Elfego Baca," *Panhandle-Plains Historical Review*, 56(1984):1-12; Pat Henry, "Elfego Baca: Century-Old Legend Merges into Folklore," *El Paso Times*, 7 October 1984. For a recent item which uses the *Albuquerque Evening Democrat* coverage of the Frisco Plaza incident, see Mike Hayes, "Elfego Baca and the Frisco Shootout," *Old West* 26(Spring 1990):30-34, 39-40. See also the Napoleon B. Laughlin Papers, folder 115, New Mexico State Records Center and Archives, Santa Fe (hereafter cited as NMSRCA).

For Elfego Baca's ancestry and early life, see *Here Comes Elfego!*, 9); baptismal data are in the Socorro Book of Baptisms, 1854-1865 (Letter, Marina Ochoa, archivist, Historic-Artistic Patrimony and Archives of the Archdiocese of Santa Fe, New Mexico, 16 May 1991). For the earliest published sketches of Elfego Baca, see *An Illustrated History of New Mexico* (Chicago: Lewis Pub. Co., 1895), 433-34, and *Albuquerque Morning Journal*, 25 February 1912 (New Mexico Historical and Resources

Edition). For some family recollections of Elfego Baca's nephew, Abe B. Baca, see *Albuquerque Journal*, 15 November 1981, clipping copy in the Socorro Public Library, Socorro, N. Mex.; F. Stanley (Crocchiola), *The Duke City: The Story of Albuquerque, New Mexico, 1706-1956* (Pampa, Tex.: Pampa Print Shop, 1963), 208, says the Baca residence was located on the corner of the plaza and Bernard Street in Socorro. For Jose Baca, see U. S., Department of Commerce, Bureau of the Census, *Ninth Census of the United States*, 1870, Socorro County, N. Mex., Population Schedules, National Archives Microcopy M593, roll 896; Francisco Baca is given the additional name, "y Volarde," in the *Daily New Mexican* (hereafter cited as DNM), 31 December 1880; the village of San Marcial, early home of Bacas, was abandoned to the floodwaters of the Elephant Butte Lake project (J. Evetts Haley, *Jeff Milton: A Good Man with a Gun* [Norman: University of Oklahoma, 1953], 103).

[2]Crichton, *Law and Order, Ltd.*, 5-8; U. S., Department of Commerce, Bureau of the Census, *Eighth Census of the United States*, Socorro County, N. Mex., National Archives Microcopy M653, roll 714, lists Francisco Baca, his wife, Juana, and two children, Nestor (age four) and Abdenago (age one year). A fifth person, Cenobio Garcia (age twelve), also resided in the household; *Albuquerque Journal*, 15 November 1981, for Abe Baca's recollections.

[3]*Here Comes Elfego!*, 9-10; Crichton, *Law and Order, Ltd.*, 7-8; *Albuquerque Journal*, 15 November 1981; Charles Curtis attended elementary and high school in Topeka in the 1870s. He also became a locally noted jockey at the same time, according to William E. Unrau, who is writing a biography of Curtis (Unrau to the author, 23 October 1990); information about the Oakland community provided by the Kansas Historical Society, Topeka. No reference to Elfego Baca's stay in Topeka has been found in the files of the society. An examination of the 1870 and 1880 censuses for Shawnee County (Topeka), Kan., failed to reveal any mention of the Francisco Baca family.

[4]*Here Comes Elfego!*, 11; Crichton, *Law and Order, Ltd.*, 7-8, 214-17; Michel D. Abousleman, comp., *Who's Who in New Mexico* (Albuquerque: Abousleman, 1937), 15-16, s. v. "Elfego Baca," for the comment about his lack of education; the death

records of the Catholic Church in Topeka have unfortunately not survived for the period in which the Bacas resided there.

[5]Crichton, *Law and Order, Ltd.*, 8; Elfego Baca's name does not appear in 1880 census for Socorro County (Bureau of the Census, *Tenth Census of the United States*, Socorro County, 1880, NA Micro. T9, roll 804).

[6]*Here Comes Elfego!*, 10-12; Robert K. DeArment, "The Blood-Spattered Trail of Milton J. Yarberry," *Old West* 22(Fall 1985):8-15, for a well researched account.

[7]*Here Comes Elfego!*, pp. 13-14; *DNM* (Santa Fe), 26 May 1882, for mention of Deputy Sheriff Cornelio Murphy on official business; DeArment, "The Blood-Spattered Trail," 8-15.

[8]*Here Comes Elfego!*, 13-14.

[9]Robert M. Utley, *Billy the Kid: A Short and Violent Life* (Lincoln: University of Nebraska, 1989), 250, n. 15, for some discussion of the confusion about various "Kids" in Albuquerque; *DNM*, 9 March 1883, for the "Slim Kid"; Jeff C. Dykes, *Billy the Kid: The Bibliography of a Legend*, University of New Mexico Publications in Language and Literature, no. 7 (Albuquerque: University of New Mexico, 1952), 65-66, doubts Baca's association with Billy the Kid; Ramon F. Adams, *A Fitting Death for Billy the Kid* (Norman: University of Oklahoma, 1960), 232-33, agrees with Dykes.

[10]*Here Comes Elfego!*, 14, for employment at Barelas; *Tenth Census of the United States*, 1880, Bernalillo County, N. Mex., NA Micro. T9, roll 802, for Francisco and Pedro Apodaca.

[11]*DNM*, 11, 31 December 1880, 2 February 1881. In the 1880 census, these brothers are apparently Otimio (age twenty-five) and Saturnino (age twenty-two), both sheepherders (*Tenth Census of the United States*, Valencia County, N. Mex., NA Micro. T9, roll 804), *DNM*, 13, 29 May, 26 June 1881.

[12]*DNM*, 13, 29 May, 26 June 1881.

[13]Crichton, *Law and Order, Ltd.*, 8-14, 154-55, relates Baca's version of the jailbreak. Baca mistakenly places the escape on St. Theresa's festival day, or 15 October. Baca later took interested persons to see the old courthouse and jail building, which became the Los Lunas Hotel; William A. Keleher, *The Fabulous Frontier: Twelve New Mexico Items* (Albuquerque: University of New Mexico, 1962), 61-62, for Thomas F. Conway as attorney

for one of New Mexico's cattle kings, John Chisum; archivists at NMSRCA searched the District Court Records for Valencia County but failed to find any documents pertinent to this case.

[14]*DNM*, 26 June 1881.

[15]Crichton, *Law and Order, Ltd.*, 13-15; in 1880, Juan Jose Baca, merchant, age 37, and his wife, Francisca, age 30, resided in Socorro with their six children (*Tenth Census of the United States*, Socorro County, N. Mex., NA Micro. T9, roll 804); see the reference to reading law at this early date in the biographical sketch (*Albuquerque Morning Journal*, 25 February 1912).

[16]For some references to Pedro Simpson, see *DNM*, 27 January, 25 March 1883, *Weekly New Mexican*, 6, 13 September 1883, *Silver City Enterprise*, 20 April 1883; Crichton, *Law and Order, Ltd.*, 69-71.

[17]For Baca's recollections of this event, see Janet Smith, "Interview with Elfego Baca: The Manzano Gang," 7 pp. ms., n. d., Works Projects Administration interview, History Folder 87, NMSRCA; Smith had a second session, "Interview with Elfego Baca: Outlaws, Joe Fowler, Henry Coleman," 27 July 1936, Folder 88, 6 pp.; *DNM*, 27 January 1883.

[18]*DNM*, 27 January 1883; Frank Collinson, *Life in the Saddle*, Mary Whatley Clarke, ed. (Norman: University of Oklahoma Press, 1963), 217-18; "Interview with Elfego Baca," WPA Interview no. 87, NMSRCA.

[19]Pedro Sarracino, his wife, and son, resided in Limitar, just north of Socorro (*Tenth Census of the United States*, Socorro County, N. Mex., NA Micro. T9, roll 804); William French, *Some Recollections of a Western Ranchman, New Mexico: 1883-1899* (London: Methuen, 1927), 42-43, believed that Baca was electioneering; "Interview with El Fego Baca," WPA Interview: The Manzano Gang, NMSRCA); Abe B. Baca asserted that his uncle went to see a girlfriend (clipping, *Albuquerque Journal*, 15 November 1981); *Albuquerque Morning Journal*, 25 February 1912.

[20]*An Illustrated History of New Mexico*, 433-34, and the *Albuquerque Morning Journal*, 25 February 1912, make straightforward references to Elfego as deputy of Sheriff Simpson; the story of Baca's "self-made deputyship" first appears in writing in the 1920s (*Here Comes Elfego!*, 16-17); see the commission in

Territory v. *Elfego Baca*, Napoleon B. Laughlin Papers, NM-SRCA, Folder no. 115; Smith, "Interview with Elfego Baca," WPA interview no. 87, NMSRCA. Some uncertainty exists about the timing of this document. Given the informality in these frontier sheriffs' offices, it is possible that Sheriff Pedro Simpson gave Elfego Baca a verbal commission and then later wrote out the document. If Elfego had a girlfriend in San Francisco Plaza, the most likely candidate would be Anamaria, daughter of his friend, Geronimo Armijo. She would have been about seventeen in 1884 (Bureau of the Census, *Tenth Census of the United States*, Socorro County, NA Micro. T9).

[21]*Here Comes Elfego!*, 16-17; that the trip took some time is apparent from Baca's statement that the return trip to Socorro "took all of the night and the better part of the next day" (*Law and Order, Ltd.*, 46).

[22]Haley, *Jeff Milton*, 103-20, and French, *Some Recollections*, 14-38, for the geography and economic enterprises in western Socorro County; see also James H. Cook, *Fifty Years on the Old Frontier, As Cowboy, Hunter, Guide, Scout, and Ranchman* (1923; reprint, Norman: University of Oklahoma, 1957), 139-42.

[23]Jack D. Rittenhouse, "Introduction," Beckett, *Baca's Battle*, 5-12; Upper San Francisco Plaza is now Reserve, Catron County, N. Mex. Middle and Lower Plazas still retain their separate identities; James Logan, age 43, born in Scotland, gave his occupation as a miner. His wife, Josefa, age 33, and son Pablo, 13, were members of the household (*Tenth Census of the United States*, Socorro County, NA Micro. T9, roll 804); Some confusion exists about the identity of Milligan. William French, *Some Recollections*, 21, calls him Dan, while he is called W. R. elsewhere. This Milligan may be a different person, since the 1870 census lists him as residing in Contadera, far to the east on the Rio Grande (*Ninth Census of the United States*, Socorro County, NA Micro. 593, roll 896); no Milligan is recorded at San Francisco Plaza in the 1880 enumeration; although four separate households of Lopezes were listed in the Plaza, the justice of the peace may have been Manuel Lopez (Lopes), age 27 in 1880, and a farmer. The other Lopezes were younger.

[24]French, *Some Recollections*, 35-36. The victim, Gereen,

could possibly be a Giron. The 1880 census for San Francisco Plaza records Alejo Giron, age 50, farmer and stock raiser, with a large family, including sons Gregorio, age 23, David, age 22, and Abran, age 16 (*Tenth Census of the United* States, Socorro County, NA Micro. T9, roll 804); *Rocky Mountain News* (Denver), 17 May 1884; Baca, *Here Comes Elfego!*, 15-16.

[25]French, *Some Recollections*, 42-43; Thorp, "Elfego Baca," WPA Files, no. 88, NMSRCA; Collinson, *Life in the Saddle*, 215-18, mistakenly says the sheriff killed three cowboys; *Las Vegas Daily Gazette* (New Mexico), 23 January 1883, reported only one cowboy killed; for the lynching of Joel Fowler, which caused considerable comment, see F. Stanley (Crocchiola), *Desperadoes of New Mexico* (Denver: World Press, 1953), chap. 15, 261-73.

[26]James H. Cook, *Fifty Years On the Old Frontier,* (1923; reprint, Norman: University of Oklahoma Press, 1957); William French, *Some Recollections* (London: Methuen & Co., 1927); J. Evetts Haley interviewed Montague Stevens, Albuquerque, N. Mex., 11 April 1946 (copy on file, Nita Stewart Haley Library, Midland, Tex.); for Alfred Hardcastle's recollections, see the excerpts from a letter to Kyle Crichton and reprinted in *Law and Order, Ltd.*, 64-67; the *Black Range's* reports are available in V. B. Beckett, *Baca's Battle: Elfego Baca's Epic Gunfight at 'Frisco Plaza, N. M., 1884, as Reported at the Time, Together with Baca's Own Final Account of the Battle*, Jack D. Rittenhouse, ed. (Houston, Texas: Stagecoach Press, 1962). This work also contains that portion of Elfego Baca's *Political Record* pertinent to the Frisco affair; Laughlin Papers, NMSRCA, Santa Fe.

[27]Baca's testimony, *Albuquerque Evening Democrat*, 9 May 1885; Abe B. Baca, Elfego's nephew, recalled hearing his uncle say that he arrived about 2 p.m. and that a "Spanish lady was coming out of church and they [cowboys] roped her and dragged her" (clipping, *Albuquerque Journal*, 15 November 1981, Socorro Public Library).

[28]Ibid.; McCarthy and Parham were cowhands for John B. and William B. Slaughter in Texas (Haley, *Jeff Milton*, 110 n. 8.).

[29]Haley, *Jeff Milton*, 110.

[30]Ibid.; Baca, *Here Comes Elfego!*, 18.

[31]*The Black Range* (Chloride), 14 November 1884, in Beck-

ett, *Baca's Battle*, 13-20; "Young" was Parham's Christian name; Cook, *Fifty Years*, 223.

[32]Baca, *Here Comes Elfego!*, 18; in the Naranjo household, there were two Franciscos, enumerated as I and II. Their relationship is unclear. Elfego Baca's friend was probably Francisco I, age 26, and a farmer (*Tenth Census of the United States*, Socorro County, NA Micro. T9, roll 804). The names of the possemen are not definitely known, but were probably the same as the defendants later charged with Elfego in the death of William Parham. These included Pedro Sarracino, Francisquito, Quico and Chi Naranjo, Bernard Chavez, Juan Luna, Jose Andres, and Patrocinio Romero (Hayes, "Elfego Baca and the Frisco Shootout," 31-34, 39-40). Some of the above are listed in the 1880 census: Chi Naranjo may be Cris Naranjo, age 23, and a farmer; Bernard Chavez may be Bernabe Chavez, age 30, farmer and stock raiser; Juan Luna, age 40, farmer and stock raiser, and Patrocinio Romero, age 20, residing at home.

[33]Baca's testimony, *Albuquerque Evening Democrat*, 9 May 1885; Cook, *Fifty Years*, 221; French, *Some Recollections*, 43-44.

[34]Baca is responsible for the figure of eighty, but used one hundred elsewhere see, Baca, *Here Comes Elfego!*, 19; Cook, *Fifty Years*, 222; French, *Some Recollections*, 44; Testimony of Jerome Wadsworth, *Albuquerque Evening Democrat*, 8 May 1885; obituary, *Las Cruces Sun News*, 28 August 1945.

[35]French, *Some Recollections*, 44-45; Baca, *Here Comes Elfego*, 19.

[36]French, *Some Recollections*, 44; Cook, *Fifty Years*, 224, relies upon Baca's version for some material; William W. Wilson, age 31, from Pennsylvania, with no occupation listed (*Tenth Census of the United States*, Socorro County, NA Micro. T9, roll 804).

[37]Testimony of Jerome Wadsworth, *Albuquerque Evening Democrat*, 8 May 1885; Baca's testimony, issue of 9 May; Baca, *Here Comes Elfego!*, 18-19.

[38]*Here Comes Elfego!*, 19; Testimony of Jerome Wadsworth, *Albuquerque Evening Democrat*, 8 May 1885; no name similar to J. Parozia is in the 1880 census. Reyes Pacheco, age 20, at home, and Fernando Peralta, age 50, a farmer, are possibilities

(*Tenth Census of the United States*, Socorro County, NA Micro. T9, roll 804).

[39]Baca's testimony, *Albuquerque Evening Democrat*, 9 May 1885; Baca, *Here Comes Elfego!*, 19-20; Cook, *Fifty Years*, 224; French, *Some Recollections*, 46; Geronimo (also spelled Jeronimo) Armijo, age 26, stock raiser, with Josefa, wife, and five children (*Tenth Census of the United States*, Socorro County, NA Micro. T9, roll 804).

[40]*Tenth Census of the United States*, Socorro County, NA Micro. T9, roll 804; Cook, *Fifty Years*, 224; Testimony of Baca and Wadsworth, *Albuquerque Evening Democrat*, 8-9 May 1885; see also statement of John W. Shaw, defense attorney for Elfego Baca, to the court, in ibid., 7 May 1885.

[41]French, *Some Recollections*, 45-46.

[42]Ibid.; Testimony of Jerome Wadsworth, *Albuquerque Evening Democrat*, 8 May 1885; Justice of the Peace William Wilson issued a warrant for the arrest of Baca on 1 November 1884. Wilson apparently gave Hearne and his posse verbal authority to arrest Baca and later went through the formality of paperwork. See the warrant, Laughlin Papers, folder 115, NMSRCA. Hearne's name is spelled many ways: Hern, Herne, Hurn, and Hearne. The latter spelling is used on the warrant and other court documents and is used in this paper. His full name was apparently William Burton Hearne.

[43]French, *Some Recollections*, 46-47; Bill McGaw, "Stories about Elfego Baca Standing Off 80 Men Are a 'Lot of Nonsense,' N. M. Rancher Says," undated clipping reprinted on front endsheet, Crichton, *Law and Order, Ltd.*.

[44]Testimony of Jerome Wadsworth, *Albuquerque Evening Democrat*, 8 May 1885.

[45]Testimony of Baca, *Albuquerque Evening Democrat*, 9 May 1885; Baca, *Here Comes Elfego!*, 20; Molo was evidently a nickname for one of Geronimo Armijo's three sons, Joaquin, age 9, Esequiel, age 7, or Rubin, age 3 (*Tenth Census of the United States*, Socorro County, NA Micro. T9, roll 804).

[46]Testimony of Baca, *Albuquerque Evening Democrat*, 9 May 1885.

[47]Testimony of Jerome Wadsworth and O. B. Bishop, *Albuquerque Evening Democrat*, 8 May 1885.

[48]Testimony of A. M. Loftiss and O. B. Bishop, *Albuquerque Evening Democrat*, 8, 9 May 1885. Bishop's name is spelled Bission at one place in the newspaper account of the trial.

[49]Testimony of Jerome Wadwsorth, *Albuquerque Evening Democrat*, 8 May 1885.

[50]See warrant issued by Justice of the Peace William W. Wilson, 1 November 1884, Laughlin Papers, NMSRCA.

[51]Baca, *Here Comes Elfego!*, 20-21; Crichton, *Law and Order, Ltd.*, 39; *Black Range*, 14 November 1884, in Beckett, *Baca's Battle*, 13-20; clipping, *Albuquerque Evening Journal*, 15 November 1981, Socorro Public Library.

[52]Baca, *Here Comes Elfego!*, 20-21; Cook, *Fifty Years*, pp. 224-25; French, *Some Recollections*, 46-47.

[53]Hardcastle's recollections, Crichton, *Law and Order, Ltd.*, 65-67.

[54]French, *Some Recollections*, 48-49; Crichton, *Law and Order, Ltd.*, 39-40.

[55]Cook, *Fifty Years*, 225; Crichton, *Law and Order, Ltd.*, 37-39; French, *Some Recollections*, 50-51; *Black Range*, 14 November 1884, in Beckett, *Baca's Battle*, 13-20.

[56]French, *Some Recollections*, 50-51.

[57]Cook, *Fifty Years*, 225.

[58]Ibid., 226; Baca, *Here Comes Elfego!*, 21; French, *Some Recollections*, 51.

[59]Baca, *Here Comes Elfego!*, 21; Cook, *Fifty Years*, 226;

[60]French, *Some Recollections*, 51; Crichton, *Law and Order, Ltd.*, 43, 63.

[61]Hardcastle's recollections, Crichton, *Law and Order, Ltd.*, 66-67; Cook, *Fifty Years*, 226; Elfego Baca later asserted that the siege lasted thirty-six hours, but the sources indicate a lesser figure (*Here Comes Elfego!*, 20).

[62]*Here Comes Elfego!*, 226; French, *Some Recollections*, 51-52; Smith, "Interview with Elfego Baca: The Manzano Gang," WPA interview no. 87, NMSRCA.

[63]Baca, *Here Comes Elfego!*, 21; Testimony of Baca, *Albuquerque Evening Democrat*, 9 May 1885.

[64]Haley, *Jeff Milton*, 111-14.

[65]Ibid.

[66]*Territory of New Mexico v. Elfego Baca*, Laughlin Papers, folder 115, NMSRCA, *Albuquerque Evening Democrat*, 6-11 May 1885; *Daily Optic* (Las Vegas, N. Mex.), 6, 9, 13 May 1885; *The Chronicle* (Las Vegas), 29 November 1884; trial, *Silver City Enterprise*, 11 December 1885; *Daily New Mexican* (Santa Fe), 13, 25 March, 3 April 1886; *Black Range*, 14 November 1884, in Beckett, *Baca's Battle*, 13-20.

[67]French, *Some Recollections*, 52.

[68]*An Illustrated History of New Mexico* (Santa Fe: n. p., 1912), 433-34; *Albuquerque Morning Journal* (New Mexico Historical Edition), 25 February 1912; For Santiago Baca's business and civic activities see, Marc Simmons, *Albuquerque: A Narrative History* (Albuquerque: University of New Mexico, 1982), 208-9, 230, 235, 298.

[69]The 1880 census list Joseph Pohmer, age 55, a baker, born in Bavaria, Dolores, his wife, age 15, Jose, his son, age 15, and Francisca, daughter, age 11, and Santiago Baca, age 37, stock raiser, Piedad (?), age 32, Francisca, age 16, and Armelia, age 2 (*Tenth Census of the United States*, Bernalillo County, NA Micro. T9, roll 802); F. Stanley, *The Duke City* (Pampa, Tex.: Pampa Print Shop, 1963), 31, 44, 175. See Ibid., 27, 39, for advertisement of Joseph Pohmer's Pioneer Bakery, and 113, for Frances Pohmer's enrollment in the Albuquerque Academy's first class, in 1879.

[70]Crichton, *Law and Order, Ltd.*, 78-80; Constance Connor Modrall, *Courtroom Humor and a Selection of New Mexico Profiles* (Albuquerque: Calvin Horn, 1974), 40-41 for a variation of this episode; Abe B. Baca became a respected public servant in Socorro and held the responsible position of tax assessor for fifteen years (*Here Comes Elfego!*, 10).

[71]*Silver City Enterprise*, 24 September 1886, 11 February 1887; *Weekly New Mexican* (Santa Fe), 25 November 1886, 19 May 1887; John F. Pearce, pioneer Albuquerque physician who treated McGuire, recalled this episode (*Albuquerque Morning Journal*, 17 January 1912.)

[72]*Albuquerque Morning Democrat*, 11 September 1889; Crichton, *Law and Order, Ltd.*, 200-20l.

[73]*Socorro Times*, 31 October 1888, reprinted in Phil Cooke, ed., *Press of the Territorian*, Santa Fe, 1(October 1961).

[74]*DNM*, 30 October 1893; *Here Comes Elfego!*, 4-5; *Albuquerque Morning Journal*, 25 February 1912.

[75]The beginnings of Elfego Baca's law studies are unclear. Abe B. Baca, Elfego's nephew, believed that he had already begun to read some law before the Frisco encounter (clipping, *Albuquerque Journal*, 15 November 1981, Socorro Public Library); the biographical sketch in the *Albuquerque Morning Journal*, 25 February 1912, makes the same assertion; William A. Keleher, *New Mexicans I Knew: Memoirs, 1892-1969* (1969; reprint, Albuquerque: University of New Mexico, 1983), 179; *DNM* (Santa Fe), 13 July 1892. The issue of 28 July 1895, noted that Baca had passed the bar; Crichton, *Law and Order, Ltd.*, 198-99; Ralph Emerson Twitchell, *Leading Facts of New Mexican History*, 2 vols. (1912; reprint, Albuquerque: Horn & Wallace, 1963), 2:516 n. 435, for Hamilton; see *DNM*, 20 January 1896, for Baca's legal advertisement; Baca was not listed in the bar minutes until 1912 (*Twenty-Sixth Session of the New Mexico Bar Association, 1912* [Albuquerque: Albright & Anderson, 1912], 59).

[76]*Rio Grande Republican* (Las Cruces), 24 April 1896; *Albuquerque Morning Democrat*, 20 May 1896.

[77]Howard R. Lamar, *The Far Southwest, 1846-1912: A Territorial History* (New York: W. W. Norton, 1970), 167-69, 178, 182, 187-89; *Here Comes Elfego!*, 5; Bessie Cavanaugh to Baca, n. d., 1931, reprinted in Margaret Ward, *Cimarron Saga* (n. p., n. d.), 36-37; Stanley, *Duke City*, 113, for Frances Pohmer at the academy.

[78]*DNM*, 1 June 1895, for the capture of Jose Chavez y Chavez. This item does not mention Baca as the captor, but only that Sheriff Holm O. Bursum brought the fugitive to the Socorro jail; for Chavez's criminal career, see Manuel C. de Baca, *Vicente Silva and His 40 Bandits*, trans. Charles Aranda (Las Vegas, N. Mex.: n.p., n. d.), 49; George Curry, *George Curry, 1861-1947: An Autobiography*, ed. H. B. Hening (Albuquerque: University of New Mexico, 1958), 36, 102-3, 116.

[79]Marc Simmons, "Elfego Baca," *Reader's Encyclopedia of The American West* (New York: Thomas Y. Crowell, 1977), 66; Keleher, *New Mexicans I Knew*, 153-64, for Baca's business card.

[80]*DNM*, 27 July 1893; Victor Westphall, *Thomas Benton Catron and His Era* (Tucson: University of Arizona, 1973), chap. 12, 208-29, see 214, for Baca's tip.

[81]Leon C. Metz, *Pat Garrett: The Story of a Western Lawman* (Norman: University of Oklahoma, 1974), 180; Arrell M. Gibson, *The Life and Death of Colonel Albert Jennings Fountain* (Norman: University of Oklahoma, 1965), 229-31.

[82]Keleher, *The Fabulous Frontier*, 241 n. 3; Metz, *Pat Garrett*, 180; W. B. S. [John C. Fraser] to William Pinkerton, 19 April 1896, enc. in Pinkerton to William Thornton, 23 April 1896, copy in Katherine Stoes Papers, Rio Grande Collection, New Mexico State University, Las Cruces.

[83]*Albuquerque Daily Citizen*, 29, 30 November, 1, 2, 5 December 1898, 5, 18, 26 January, 20 February, 4 March 1899; *New York Times*, 1 February, 24, 25, 27, 30 May 1904; Crichton, *Law and Order, Ltd.*, 114-15; information about the background of the Grant Gillett case provided by the Kansas Historical Society Topeka, Kansas (telephone conversation, Jane Kelsey, 8 October 1990).

[84]Crichton, *Law and Order, Ltd.*, 114-15; *DNM*, 8 July 1895, for Charles Hunt's resignation.

[85]*New York Times*, 11 August 1904; Crichton, *Law and Order, Ltd.*, 114-15.

[86]*DNM*, [?] January 1908, quoted in *Socorro Chieftain*, 11 January 1908; see also *Chieftain*, 6 June 1908, 6 February, 26 June, 3, 17, 24 July, 14 August, 4, 18 September, 27 November 1909, 26 March, 2 April, 24 September 1910, for reports of Baca's cases; *Albuquerque Morning Journal*, 25 February 1912.

[87]Philip J. Rasch, "An Incomplete Account of 'Broncho Bill' Walters," *English Westerners' Brand Book* 19(January 1977): 1-12; Howard Bryan, *Robbers, Rogues and Ruffians: True Tales of the Wild West in New Mexico* (Santa Fe: Clear Light, 1991), 167-208, for the fullest treatment of Bronco Bill Walters.

[88]Janet Smith, "Elfego Baca," WPA Files, NMSRCA, History Folder no. 88, 27 July 1936.

[89]Baca to Secundino Romero, District Court Clerk, 8 December 1904, Elfego Baca Papers, Special Collections Department, University of New Mexico Library, Albuquerque.

[90]Agnes Morley Cleaveland, *No Life for a Lady* (1941;

reprint, Lincoln: University of Nebraska, 1977), 262-70, for Baca's defense of Corky.

[91]Joseph F. Towle to Holm O. Bursum, 23 August 1898, Bursum Papers, Spec. Coll. Dept., UNM, box 1; Miguel Antonio Otero, *My Nine Years as Governor of the Territory of New Mexico,* 1897-1906 (1940; reprint, New York: Arno, 1974), 369-71.

[92]Executive Record of the Governors of New Mexico, Book no. 6, p. 180, Territorial Archives of New Mexico, roll 23, NMSRCA; Ellen Lloyd Trover, ed., *Chronology and Documentary Handbook of the State of Arizona* (New York: Oceana, 1972), 98. The inclusion of this reference to events in New Mexico arose from the jointure proposal for the two territories. The committee members misunderstood the nature of the district attorneyship in New Mexico. Each district included two or more counties; Eugene Manlove Rhodes, "Hit the Line Hard," *The Best Novels and Stories of Eugene Manlove Rhodes*, ed. Frank V. Dearing (1910; reprint, Lincoln: University of Nebraska, 1987), 353-98. This novelette originally appeared in *The Saturday Evening Post* (27 March-3 April 1915); W. H. Hutchinson, *A Bar Cross Man: The Life and Personal Writings of Eugene Manlove Rhodes* (Norman: University of Oklahoma, 1956), 101-102, 134-37.

[93]*Albuquerque Evening Citizen*, 15 February, 27 March 1906.

[94]Ibid.

[95]Letter, Elfego Baca to editor, 29 March, 30 March 1906.

[96]E. L. Medler to Fred Fornoff, 12 December 1906, Records of the Mounted Police, Territorial Archives of New Mexico, NMSRCA, roll 91; *Here Comes Elfego!*, 5-6; *Socorro Chieftain*, 7 December 1907.

[97]*Albuquerque Evening Citizen*, 12 April, 15 May 1906. H. A. Woolford, an attorney in Hillsboro, Sierra County, succeeded Baca as district attorney.

[98]*Albuquerque Evening Citizen*, 3 July, 2 August 1906; "In The Matter of Charges Against Leandro Baca, Sheriff of Socorro County, New Mexico," 6 October 1906, Executive Record of the Governors of New Mexico, Book no. 6, pp. 366-70, Territorial Archives of New Mexico, roll 23, NMSRCA; Chuck Hornung, *The Thin Gray Line: The New Mexico*

Mounted Police (Fort Worth, Texas: Western Heritage, 1971), 47.

[99]*Albuquerque Evening Citizen*, 7 July 1906.

[100]Ibid.

[101]*Albuquerque Evening Citizen*, 29 January, 12 February, 1906.

[102]Ibid., 17, 24 July 1906.

[103]*Albuquerque Evening Journal*, 25 February 1912; *Socorro Chieftain*, 23 May 1908, 5 March 1910; Porter A. Stratton, *The Territorial Press of New Mexico, 1834-1912* (Albuquerque: University of New Mexico Press, 1969), 59, 65-66; Annabelle M. Ozcon, "Bilingual and Spanish-Language Newspapers in Territorial New Mexico," *New Mexico Historical Review* 54(January 1979):45-52.

[104]*Albuquerque Morning Journal*, 7 December 1907; for the Hispanic-American Alliance see E. B. Fincher, *Spanish-Americans as a Political Factor in New Mexico, 1912-1950* (New York: Arno, 1974), 89-90; *Albuquerque Evening Citizen*, 25 February 1912; Curry,*autobiography,* 222-24, for the Irrigation Congress, which was held in conjunction with the territorial fair.

[105]*Albuquerque Citizen*, [?] May 1908, reprinted in *Socorro Chieftain*, 9 May 1908.

[106]Ibid.

[107]*Socorro Chieftain*, 14 November, 12 December 1908, 6 March 1909; Crichton, *Law and Order, Ltd.*, pp. 200-20l.

[108]*Socorro Chieftain*, 7 December 1907, 1 February 1908.

[109]Twitchell, *Leading Facts,* 2:594-603; Curry, *autobiography*, 258-62.

[110]Curry, Ibid, 258-62; Twitchell, *Leading Facts*, 2:602 n. for final count of votes; Benjamin M. Read, *Illustrated History of New Mexico*, trans. from the 2d Spanish ed. (Santa Fe: New Mexican, 1911; reprint ed., New York: Arno, 1976), 624-26. Voters expressed their will in this issue on blue paper, hence the Blue Ballot Amendment (Stratton, *Territorial Press of New Mexico*, 113-14).

[111]*La Opinion Publica*, [?] November 1911, reprinted in *Albuquerque Evening Journal*, 15 November 1911; Stratton, *Territorial Press of New Mexico*, 114-5 and n. 166.

[112]Read, *Illustrated History*, 642-44 and note. The accused

were Manuel Cordova and Luis R. Montoya of Taos County and J. P. Lucero and Julian Trujillo of Rio Arriba County; *Socorro Chieftain*, 23 March 1912.

[113]Unidentified newspaper quoted in Read, *Illustrated History*, 643 n.; *Here Comes Elfego!*, 6; Crichton, *Law and Order, Ltd.*, 178-79, for the election of Fall. On p. 199 Baca says he was admitted to the U. S. Supreme Court in 1919.

[114]Author Interview with Mary Foraker, Albuquerque, 12 August 1976.

[115]Elfego Baca to Fred Fornoff, 21 December 1909, Records of the Mounted Police, Territorial Archives of New Mexico, roll 91, NMSRCA.

[116]*DNM*, 11 September 1891; Westphall, *Thomas Benton Catron*, 171-72; Catron also made loans and gifts of money to Baca (ibid., 388 n.); *Socorro Chieftain*, 18 September 1909, for building in Socorro, and issue of 26 August 1911 for one in Albuquerque; *1914 City Directory* (copy provided by Bob Dauner, Albuquerque Public Library).

[117]*Albuquerque Morning Journal*, 2, 6, 15 March 1912; *Here Comes Elfego!*, 6.

[118]Keleher, *New Mexicans I Knew*, 153-54.

[119]Crichton, *Law and Order, Ltd.*, 115-29.

[120]Ibid., 130-49, for Baca's recollections of the Salazar affair; Ralph H. Vigil, "Revolution and Confusion: The Peculiar Case of Jose Ynez Salazar," *New Mexico Historical* Review 53(April 1978):145-70, provides a well-researched account; Oliver La Farge, *Santa Fe: The Autobiography of a Southwestern Town* (Norman: University of Oklahoma, 1959), 217-20; *El Paso Herald*, 12 April 1915; *Dictionary of American Biography*, supp. 1, for sketch of Hugh Lenox Scott; Hugh Lenox Scott, *Some Memories of a Soldier* (New York: Century, 1928), does not mention the encounter with Elfego Baca, but see between pp. 488 and 489 for photo of General Salazar in Fort Bliss internment camp.

[121]*New York Times*, 15 March 1914.

[122]Vigil, "Revolution and Confusion," 145-70; *New York Times*, 22 November 1914; Crichton, *Law and Order, Ltd.*, 134-45, for Baca's version of the jailbreak.

[123]*New York Times*, 8 December 1914; La Farge, *Santa Fe*, 219. In addition to Elfego Baca, the indictees were: District At-

torney Manuel U. Vigil, State Game Warden Trinidad C. de Baca, Monico Aranda, Deputy Sheriff Carlos Armijo, and one Porfirio, alias Perfilio Savedra. Celestino Otero, another alleged conspirator, had been killed by Elfego Baca.

[124]Vigil, "Revolution and Confusion," 145-70.

[125]Crichton, *Law and Order, Ltd.*, 132-33; George Fitzpatrick, "The Real Elfego Baca," *New Mexico Magazine* 38(April 1960):2-6, 40, pt. 1.

[126]Crichton, *Law and Order, Ltd.*, chap. 13, 150-58; *El Paso Herald*, 1 February 1915; Pat Henry, "South-of-the-Border Ties Link Elfego to El Paso," *El Paso Times*, 7 October 1984; *Times-Picayune*, 2 February 1915.

[127]*El Paso Herald*, 1 February 1915. In the 1940s, J. R. Galusha, a veteran New Mexico lawman and acquaintance of Elfego Baca, informed Howard Bryan that he had traveled to El Paso to investigate the Otero shooting. Galusha asserted that Elfego had purchased a pistol at a pawn shop and placed it on Otero's body (telephone interview with Howard Bryan, 19 June 1991).

[128]Crichton, *Law and Order, Ltd.*, 151-54.

[129]Ibid., 154-58.

[130]Vigil, "Revolution and Confusion," 145-70; Baca later boasted that he used an "ocular barrage," that is, staring down individual jurors as a means to intimidate them (Crichton, *Law and Order, Ltd.*, 156-58).

[131]Vigil, "Revolution and Confusion," 145-70; Crichton, *Law and Order, Ltd.*, 135-36; Galusha recounted his story about Elfego's alibi to Howard Bryan (interview with Howard Bryan, 16 June 1991).

[132]Curry, *Autobiography*, 69; *El Paso Herald*, 17 February 1916; see Larry D. Ball, "The Frontier Sheriff's Role in Law and Order," *Western Legal History* 4(Winter/Spring 1991):13-25, for some general observations about this office.

[133]*Here Comes Elfego!*, 6-7; Crichton, *Law and Order, Ltd.*, chap. 8, 83-98, chap. 9, 99-111, for Baca's experiences as sheriff. Author Crichton arranged these chapters out of chronological order, placing them immediately after Baca's experiences as a deputy sheriff twenty-five years earlier. Apparently Crichton believed that readers expected Baca to make the logical step to the sheriff's office immediately after serving as deputy.

[134]*Here Comes Elfego!*, 7.

[135]*The Evening Herald* (Albuquerque), 4 January 1919; Oscar Caudill, as Told to Eve Ball, "Hell on the Largo," *Frontier Times*, new series, 46(December-January 1972):6-9, 40-42; Bourbonnaise's name was misspelled variously, Burboni, Burbonde, and Borboney.

[136]*Evening Herald*, 4, 18 January 1919.

[137]Arthur Thomas Hannett, *Sagebrush Lawyer* (New York: Pageant, 1964), 12-15; Crichton, *Law and Order, Ltd.*, 107-11; Henry Coleman is referred to as Street Hudspeth, alias Henry Coleman, in a cattle theft case (*Socorro Chieftain*, 23 April 1921); Curry, *Autobiography*, 286-87, recalls the Coleman case; *Biographical Directory of the American Congress, 1774-1972* (Washington, D. C: Government Printing Office, 1971), 1055, s. v. Claude Benton Hudspeth; New Mexico Pioneers Foundation Interview with Henry Brock and John Cox, 11 April 1953, transcript in University of New Mexico Library; Henry Coleman advertised six saddle horses lost near Deming in 1908 (Chuck Hornung, *The Thin Grey Line*, 163); *DNM*, 7 September 1897, for a summary of the case of Israel King and Henry Coleman in Mexico.

[138]Caudill, "Hell on the Largo," 6-9, 40-42; *Evening Herald*, 18 January 1919.

[139]Curry, *Autobiography*, 286; interview with Howard Bryan, Albuquerque, New Mexico, 19 June 1991. The author is grateful for Bryan's assistance in researching the Henry Coleman case.

[140]Caudill, "Hell on the Largo," 42; *Socorro Chieftain*, 8 January 1921; Curry, *Autobiography*, 286-87.

[141]Curry, *Autobiography*, 287.

[142]Caudill, "Hell on the Largo," 6-9, 40-42; *Socorro Chieftain*, 23 April 1921.

[143]Caudill, "Hell on the Largo," 6-9, 40-42; Howard Bryan Interview, 19 June 1991.

[144]N. Mex. Pioneers Foundation Interview, Henry Brock and John Cox, 11 April 1953.

[145]*Evening Herald*, 25 November 1919; Janet Smith, "Interview with Elfego Baca: The Manzano Gang," Works Projects Administration Interview, no. 87, 7 pp., n. d., NMSRCA.

[146]Ibid.; *Evening Herald*, 29 November 1919.

[147]Ibid., 23 August 1919; Bernalillo County had an increase in automobiles from 1,136 to 1,580 in one year (*Evening Herald*, 21 August 1919); see ibid., 10 March 1919, for the airline's planned stopover in Socorro.

[148]Ibid., 24 July, 5 August 1919; see ibid., 8, 10 October 1919, for Sheriff Harp (also sp. Hart); Crichton, *Law and Order, Ltd.*, 199-200.

[149]*Evening Herald*, 5 September 1919.

[150]*Here Comes Elfego!*, 7-8.

[151]Crichton, *Law and Order, Ltd.*, 99-107.

[152]Hornung, *The Thin Grey Line*, esp. 53-59 and 65-68, for ups and downs of the Mounted Police; *Evening Herald*, 12 February 1919, for the lawmen's meeting; David J. McCullough, "Bone Dry? Prohibition New Mexico Style, 1918-1933," *New Mexico Historical Review* 63(January 1988):25-42.

[153]*Evening Herald*, 13 February 1919.

[154]Crichton, *Law and Order, Ltd.*, 83-84; clipping, *Albuquerque Journal*, 15 November 1981, Socorro Public Library, for Abe B. Baca's recollections.

[155]Curry, *Autobiography*, 287-89; Montague Stevens, the Englishman and rancher in western Socorro County, informed Howard Bryan that Elfego, as sheriff, paid one of his (Stevens's) sheepherders a monthly income to serve on juries and vote the way that the lawman desired (interview with Howard Bryan, 19 June 1991).

[156]Curry, *Autobiography*, 289-90.

[157]Ibid., 290.

[158]Ibid.

[159]Ibid., 290-91; Warren A. Beck and Ynez D. Haase, comps., *Historical Atlas of New Mexico* (Norman: University of Oklahoma Press, 1969), maps 51 and 52, for creation of Catron County.

[160]Crichton, *Law and Order, Ltd.*, 159-68; *Socorro Chieftain*, 18 June 1921.

[161]Crichton, *Law and Order, Ltd.*, 159-68, with photo of Baca with Mary Garden, opposite p. 160; Mary Garden and Louis Biancolli, *Mary Garden's Story* (New York: Simon and Schuster, 1951), 180-82; *New York Times*, 2 March 1921. The Chicago Grand Opera Company made a second western tour in the following year (*New York Times*, 13 April 1922).

[162]*Socorro Chieftain*, 27, 30 July, 5 November 1921, 25 February 1922.

[163]*Salt Lake Tribune*, 29, 31 May 1921; *New York Times*, 29 May 1921, also reported the Ute outbreak; Crichton, *Law and Order,Ltd.*, 304; for Elfego Baca's official correspondence, see Record Group 48, Department of Interior, Central Classified Files, 1907-1935, Indian and Land Inspectors, file No. 25, National Archives, Washington, D. C. Copies provided by the archives.

[164]Telegram, Baca to Albert B. Fall, 1 September; letter, Baca to Theodore Mack, 1 September 1921, Dept. of Int. Central Classified Files, NA; Crichton, *Law and Order, Ltd.*, 169-77; M. R. Werner and John Starr, *Teapot Dome* (New York: Viking, 1959), 39-87, for the illegal activities of Albert Fall.

[165]Crichton, *Law and Order, Ltd.*, 169-84, for Baca's thoughts about Fall; see Howard R. Lamar, *The Far Southwest, 1846-1912: A Territorial History* (New York: W. W. Norton, 1970), esp. chaps. 7 and 19, for New Mexico politics in this era; for Baca as jailer (Crichton, *Law and Order, Ltd.*, 204-9).

[166]William A. Keleher, *New Mexicans I Knew*, 186; Robert Hoath LaFollette, *Eight Notches and Other Stories of Nuevo Mejico (New Mexico) and the Land of Yaqui and Yucca (Mexico)* (Albuquerque: Valiant Printing, 1950), 4-5.

[167]Keleher, *New Mexicans I Knew*, 180-81.

[168]Crichton, *Law and Order, Ltd.*, 213-17; James C. Malin, "Charles Curtis," *Dictionary of American Biography*, supp. 2, pp. 136-37. William Unrau, biographer of Charles Curtis, finds no mention of this episode in his papers (letter to the author, 23 October 1990); U. S., *Statutes at Large*, vol. 45, pt. 1, pp. 2-50, for the Conservancy District Act.

[169]Crichton, *Law and Order, Ltd.*, 175-76, 210-14, 219; LaFollette, *Eight Notches*, 10; George Fitzpatrick, "The Real Elfego Baca," *New Mexico Magazine* 38(April 1962): 2-6, 40, pt. 1, (May 1962): 12-15, 39, pt. 2.

[170]Charles O. Paullin, "Bronson Murray Cutting," *Dictionary of American Biography*, supp. 1, pp. 215-16; for this unusual pairing of politicians, see Keleher, *New Mexicans I Knew*, 165-91; Ralph H. Vigil, ""Revolution and Confusion: The Peculiar Case of Jose Ines Salazar," *New Mexico Historical Review* 53(April 1978):145-70.

[171]Keleher, *New Mexicans I Knew*, 156; Richard Lowitt, "Bronson Cutting and the Early Years of the American Legion in New Mexico," *New Mexico Historical Review* 64(April 1989):143-58.

[172]Keleher, *New Mexicans I Knew*, 182-91; LaFollette, *Eight Notches*, 10; *El Paso Times*, 5 June 1936; Matt S. Meier and Feliciano Rivera, *Dictionary of Mexican American History* (Westport, Conn.: Greenwood, 1981), 28-29, s. v. Elfego Baca.

[173]Keleher, *New Mexicans I Knew*, 156-62, with photo of Baca with the *santo*.

[174]R. A. Gerken, Archbishop of Santa Fe, to Elfego Baca, 21 March 1938, Historic-Artistic Patrimony and Archives, Diocese of Santa Fe, Santa Fe, N. Mex.

[175]See "Manifesto of Elfego Baca, Candidate for Governor," [1934] and unid. clipping, 4 November 1940, Elfego Baca Papers, Special Collections Department, University of New Mexico Library, Albuquerque; Janet Smith, "Interview with Elfego Baca," Works Projects Administration Interviews, NMSRCA, 27 July 1936, no. 88.

[176]Telephone interview with Donald Eklund, professor of History, Western Washington State University, Bellingham, Wash., 6 October 1990.

[177]Fitzpatrick, "The Real Elfego Baca," pt. 1, p. 6.

[178]Ibid.

[179]*Albuquerque Morning Journal*, 27 November 1907; Fitzpatrick, "The Real Elfego Baca," pt. 1, pp. 2-6, 40, for observations about the literature concerning Baca; Erna Fergusson, *Our Southwest* (New York: Alfred A. Knopf, 1940), 369; W. H. Hutchinson, *A Bar Cross Man: The Life & Personal Writings of Eugene Manlove Rhodes* (Norman: University of Oklahoma, 1956), 134-37.

[180]John Armistead, "Elfego Baca: A Legend of the West," unid. clipping, Elfego Baca file, Socorro Public Library, Socorro, N. Mex.; B. A. Botkin, comp. and ed., *A Treasury of Western Folklore* (New York: Crown, 1951), pp. 375-84; "The Nine Lives of Elfego Baca," Walt Disney Productions, 1958; unid. clipping, inside back cover, Crichton, *Law and Order, Ltd.*

[181]Telephone interview with Donald Eklund, 6 October 1990.

[182]Crichton, *Law and Order, Ltd.*, 204; Carey McWilliams,

North from Mexico: The Spanish-Speaking People of the United States (1948; reprinted, New York: Greenwood, 1968), 119-21.

[183]Crichton, *Law and Order, Ltd.*, 203; Robert J. Rosenbaum, *Mexican Resistance in the Southwest: "The Sacred Law of Self-Protection"* (Austin: University of Texas, 1981), 53-60; Interview with Howard Bryan, 19 June 1991, for the reference to Baca's desire to be the subject of a movie.

[184]Cynthia Secor-Welsh, "Miguel Antonio Otero: Author and Agent for Change," introduction to Miguel Antonio Otero, *My Life on the Frontier, 1864-1882* (1935; reprint, Albuquerque: University of New Mexico, 1987), vii-lxxix. *Who's Who in New Mexico* (1937), 15-16, listed Elfego Baca as the first president, but apparently refers to the local chapter.

[185]Obituary, *Las Cruces Sun News*, 28 August 1945, copy provided by Cheryl Wilson, rare books librarian, New Mexico State University, Las Cruces, and *New York Times*, 29 August 1945; burial notice, Baca Papers, Special Collection Dept., University of New Mexico Library; Mrs. Elfego Baca to Clinton P. Anderson, U. S. Congress, 2 September 1945, in ibid.; see Elfego Baca's announcement in the *Political Record of Elfego Baca and a Brief History of His Life*, 1944, in ibid.

BIBLIOGRAPHY

Newspapers

Albuquerque Daily Citizen, 22 September 1898-31 July 1899.

Albuquerque Evening Democrat, 7, 8, 9 May 1884.

Albuquerque Evening Citizen, 1 January-16 August 1906.

Albuquerque Journal, 15 November 1881.

Albuquerque Morning Democrat, 11 September 1889, 20 May 1896.

Albuquerque Morning Journal, 17 April-27 November 1907, 1 July-26 August 1911, 1 January-25 February 1912.

Daily New Mexican (Santa Fe), 31 December 1880, 26 May, 1882, 13, 25 March 1886, 11 September 1891, 27 July 1893, 20 January 1896.

El Paso Herald, 1 February, 12 April 1915, 17 February 1916.

El Paso Times, 5 June 1936.

Evening Herald (Albuquerque), 1 November 1918-1 December 1919.

Las Cruces Sun News (New Mexico), 28 August 1945.

Las Vegas Daily Gazette (New Mexico), 23 January 1883.

Las Vegas Daily Optic (New Mexico), 6, 9, 13 May 1885.

New York Times, 1 February, 24, 25, 27, 30 May, 11 August 1904; 15 March, 24 November, 8 December 1914; 2 March, 29 May 1921; 13 April 1922; 29 August 1945.

Rio Grande Republican (Las Cruces), 24 April 1896.

Rocky Mountain News (Denver), 17 May 1884.

Salt Lake Tribune (Utah), 29, 31 May 1921.

Silver City Enterprise (New Mexico), 11 December 1885, 24 September, 11 February 1887.

Socorro Chieftain, 27 November 1907-25 May 1912, 1 January 1921-25 February 1922.

Socorro Times, 31 October 1888 (reprinted in *Press of the Territorian*. 1(October 1961).

The Chronicle (Las Vegas, New Mexico), 29 November 1884.

Times Picayune (New Orleans), 2 February 1915.

Weekly New Mexican (Santa Fe), 25 November 1886, 19 May 1887.

Unpublished Sources

Historic-Artistic Patrimony and Archives of the Archdiocese of Santa Fe

Elfego Baca Papers.

New Mexico State Records Center and Archives, Santa Fe

Executive Record of the Governors of New Mexico.

Napoleon B. Laughlin Papers.

Records of the Territorial Mounted Police, Territorial Archives of New Mexico.

Smith, Janet. "Interview with Elfego Baca: The Manzano Gang." Works Projects Administration Interview, n. d.

__________. "Interview with Elfego Baca: Outlaws, Joe Fowler, Henry Coleman." Works Projects Administration Interview, 27 July 1936.

Thorp, N. Howard. "Elfego Baca." Works Projects Administration Interview, n. d.

Nita Stewart Haley Memorial Library, Midland, Tex.

Interview, J. Evetts Haley with Montague Stevens, 11 April 1946.

Rio Grande Collection, New Mexico State University

Katherine Stoes Papers.

Socorro Public Library

Elfego Baca File.

Special Collections Department, University of New Mexico

Elfego Baca Papers.

Holm O. Bursum Papers.

New Mexico Pioneers Foundation Interviews.

U. S., Department of Commerce. Record Group 29. Bureau of the Census.

Eighth Census of the United States, 1860, Socorro County, N. Mex., National Archives Microcopy M653.

Ninth Census of the United States, 1870, Socorro County, N. Mex., National Archives Microcopy M593.

Tenth Census of the United States, 1880, Socorro, Bernalillo, and Valencia Counties, N. Mex., National Archives Microcopy T9.

U. S., Department of Interior. Record Group 48.

Central Classified Files, 1907-1935. Indian and Land Inspectors.

U.S., Statutes At Large. Vol. 45.

Published Sources

Adams, Ramon F. *A Fitting Death for Billy the Kid*. Norman: University of Oklahoma, 1960.

Baca, Elfego. *Here Comes Elfego! The Autobiography of Elfego Baca*. Albuquerque: Vinegar Tom, n. d.; orig. pub. as *Political Record of Elfego Baca and a Brief History of His Life*. [1924 ?].

Baca, Manuel C. de. *Vicente Silva and His 40 Bandits*. Translated by Charles Aranda. n. p., n. d.

Ball, Larry D. "The Frontier Sheriff's Role in Law and Order." *Western Legal History* 4(Winter/Spring 1991):13-25.

Beck, Warren A. and Ynez D. Haase. *Historical Atlas of New Mexico*. Norman: University of Oklahoma, 1969.

Beckett, V. B. *Baca's Battle: Elfego Baca's Epic Gunfight at 'Frisco Plaza, New Mexico, 1884, as Reported at the Time, Together with Baca's Own Final Account of the Battle*. Houston, Tex.: Stagecoach Press, 1962.

Biographical Directory of the American Congress, 1774-1972. Washington: Government Printing Office, 1972. s. v. "Claude Benton Hudspeth."

Botkin, B. A., comp. *A Treasury of Western Folklore*. New York: Crown, 1951.

Bryan, Howard. *Robbers, Rogues and Ruffians: True Tales of the Wild West in New Mexico*. Santa Fe: Clear Light, 1991.

Caudill, Oscar, As Told To Eve Ball. "Hell on the Largo." *Frontier Times*, New Series, 46(December 1971-January 1972):6-9, 40-42.

Cleaveland, Agnes Morley. *No Life for a Lady*. 1941. Reprint. Lincoln: University of Nebraska, 1977.

Collinson, Frank. *Life in the Saddle*. Norman: University of Oklahoma, 1963.

Cook, James H. *Fifty Years on the Old Frontier, as Cowboy, Guide, Scout, and Ranchman*. 1923. Reprint. Norman: University of Oklahoma, 1957.

Crichton, Kyle S. *Law and Order, Ltd.: The Rousing Life of Elfego Baca of New Mexico*. 1928. Reprint. Glorieta, N. Mex.: Rio Grande, 1970.

Curry, George. *George Curry, 1861-1947: An Autobiography.* Edited by H. B. Hening. Albuquerque: University of New Mexico, 1958.

Dearing, Frank V., ed. *The Best Novels and Stories of Eugene Manlove Rhodes.* Lincoln: University of Nebraska, 1987; orig. pub. 1910.

DeArment, Robert K., "The Blood-Spattered Trail of Milton J. Yarberry," *Old West* 22(Fall 1985):8-15.

Dictionary of American Biography, s. v. "Bronson Murray Cutting," "Charles Curtis," "Hugh Lenox Scott."

Dykes, Jeff C. *Billy the Kid: The Bibliography of a Legend.* University of New Mexico Publications in Language and Literature, no. 7. Albuquerque: University of New Mexico, 1952.

Fergusson, Erna. *Our Southwest.* New York: Alfred A. Knopf, 1940.

Fincher, E. B. *Spanish-Americans as a Political Factor in New Mexico, 1912-1950.* New York: Arno, 1974.

Fitzpatrick, George. "The Real Elfego Baca." *New Mexico Magazine* 38(April 1960);2-6, 40, pt. 1, (May 1960):12-15, 39, pt. 2.

French, William. *Some Recollections of a Western Ranchman, New Mexico: 1883-1899.* London: Methuen, 1927.

Garden, Mary, and Louis Biancolli. *Mary Garden's Story.* New York: Simon and Schuster, 1951.

Gibson, Arrell M. *The Life and Death of Colonel Albert Jennings Fountain.* Norman: University of Oklahoma, 1965.

Haley, J. Evetts. *Jeff Milton: A Good Man with a Gun.* Norman: University of Oklahoma, 1948.

Hannett, Arthur Thomas. *Sagebrush Lawyer.* New York: Pageant, 1964.

Hayes, Mike. "Elfego Baca and the Frisco Shootout." *Old West.* 26(Spring 1990):30-34, 39-40.

Henry, Pat. "Elfego Baca: Century-Old Legend Merges into Folklore." *El Paso Times* 7 October 1984.

__________. "South-of-the-Border Ties Link Elfego Baca to El Paso." *El Paso Times* 7 October 1984.

Hornung, Chuck. *The Thin Gray Line—The New Mexico Mounted Police.* Forth Worth: Western Heritage, 1971.

Hutchinson, W. H. *A Bar Cross Man: The Life and Personal*

Writings of Eugene Manlove Rhodes. Norman: University of Oklahoma, 1956.

An Illustrated History of New Mexico. Chicago: Lewis Pub. Co., 1895.

Johnson, Byron A. "The Rousing Life of Elfego Baca." *Panhandle-Plains Historical Review* 56(1984):1-12.

Keleher, William A. *The Fabulous Frontier: Twelve New Mexico Items*, rev. & enl. Albuquerque: University of New Mexico, 1962.

________. *New Mexicans I Knew: Memoirs, 1892-1969. 1969.* Reprint. Albuquerque: University of New Mexico, 1983.

La Farge, Oliver. *Santa Fe: The Autobiography of a Southwestern Town*. Norman: University of Oklahoma, 1959.

LaFollette, Robert Hoath. *Eight Notches and Other Stories of Nuevo Mejico (New Mexico) and the Land of Yaqui and Yucca (Mexico)*. Albuquerque: Valiant Printing, 1950.

Lamar, Howard Roberts. *The Far Southwest, 1846-1912: A Territorial History*. New York: W. W. Norton, 1970; orig. pub. 1966.

McWilliams, Carey. *North from Mexico: The Spanish Speaking People of the United States*. New York: Greenwood, 1968; orig. pub. 1948.

Meier, Matt S., and Feliciano Rivera. eds. *Dictionary of Mexican American History*. Westport, Connecticut: Greenwood, 1981.

Metz, Leon Claire. *Pat Garrett: The Story of a Western Lawman*. Norman: University of Oklahoma, 1974.

____________. *The Shooters*. El Paso, Texas: Mangan Books, 1976.

Mondrall, Constance. *Courtroom Humor and a Selection of New Mexico Profiles*. Albuquerque: Calvin Horn, 1974.

"The Nine Lives of Elfego Baca". Burbank, Calif.: Walt Disney Productions, 1958. Film.

Otero, Miguel Antonio. *My Life on the Frontier, 1864-1882*. Intro. Cynthia Secor-Welsh. 1935. Reprint. Albuquerque: University of New Mexico, 1987.

__________________. *My Nine Years as Governor of the Territory of New Mexico, 1897-1906*. Albuquerque: University of New Mexico, 1940.

Rasch, Philip J. "An Incomplete Account of 'Broncho Bill." *English Westerners' Brand Book* 19(January 1977):1-12.

Read, Benjamin M. *Illustrated History of New Mexico*. Santa Fe: New Mexican, 1911; reprint. New York: Arno, 1976. Rosenbaum, Robert J. *Mexican Resistance in the Southwest:* 'The Sacred Law of Self-Protection.' Austin: University of Texas, 1981.

Scott, Hugh Lenox. *Some Memories of a Soldier*. New York: Century, 1928.

Simmons, Marc. *Albuquerque: A Narrative History*. Albuquerque: University of New Mexico, 1982.

______________. "Elfego Baca." *Reader's Encyclopedia of the American West*. New York: Thomas Y. Crowell, 1977.

Stanley, F. (Stanley Crocchiola). *Desperadoes of New Mexico*. Denver: World Press, 1953.

___________. *The Duke City: The Story of Albuquerque, New Mexico, 1706-1956*. Pampa, Tex.: Pampa Print Shop, 1963.

Stratton, Porter A. *The Territorial Press of New Mexico, 1834-1912*. Albuquerque: University of New Mexico Press, 1969. Trover, Ellen Lloyd, ed. *Chronology and Documentary Handbook of the State of Arizona*. New York: Oceana, 1972.

Twenty-Sixth Session of the New Mexico Bar Association, 1912. Albuquerque: Albright & Anderson, 1912.

Twitchell, Ralph Emerson. *Leading Facts of New Mexican History*. 2 vols. 1917. Reprint. Albuquerque: Horn & Wallace, 1963.

Utley, Robert M. *Billy the Kid: A Short and Violent Life*. Lincoln: University of Nebraska, 1989.

Vigil, Ralph H. "Revolution and Confusion: the Peculiar Case of Jose Ines Salazar." *New Mexico Historical Review* 53(April 1978):145-70.

Walter, Paul A. F. "Octaviano Ambrosio Larrazolo." *New Mexico Historical Review*. 7(April 1932):97-104.

Ward, Margaret. *Cimarron Saga*. n. p., n. d.

Werner, M. R. and Starr, John. *Teapot Dome*. New York: Viking, 1959.

Westphall, Victor. *Thomas Benton Catron and His Era*. Tucson: University of Arizona, 1973.

Who's Who in New Mexico. Albuquerque: Michel D. Abousleman, 1937, s. v. "Elfego Baca."

Author Correspondence and Interviews

Howard Bryan, Telephone, 19 June 1991.
Donald Eklund, Telephone, 6 October 1990.
Mary Foraker, Albuquerque, N. Mex., 12 August 1976.
William, Unrau. Letter to author, 23 October 1990.

INDEX